HIDDEN
W.O.M.B.A.T.

The Needs-Driven Innovation Handbook

HIDDEN
W.O.M.B.A.T.

How Executives Innovate
without the Waste of Money, Brains, and Time

Rush Bartlett, PhD
Topher Kinsella, MD

Hidden WOMBAT copyright © 2023 by Rush Bartlett, PhD and Topher Kinsella, MD

WOMBAT Innovation
www.hiddenwombat.com

Publisher's Cataloging-in-Publication

Names: Bartlett, Rush, author. | Kinsella, Topher, author.
Title: Hidden WOMBAT : how executives innovate without the Waste of Money, Brains, and Time / Rush Bartlett, PhD, Topher Kinsella, MD.
Description: Bellevue, WA : WOMBAT Innovation, [2023] | Includes bibliographical references.
Identifiers: ISBN: 979-8-9892476-1-5 (hardcover) | 979-8-9892476-0-8 (softcover) | 979-8-9892476-2-2 (ebook) | 979-8-9892476-3-9 (audiobook)

Subjects: LCSH: New products. | Industrial design. | Technological innovations. | Marketing. | Demand (Economic theory) | Consumption (Economics) | Success in business.

Classification: LCC: HF5415.153 .B47 2023 | DDC: 658.575--dc23

Dedication

To Amy Bartlett, all in and incredible. To our Boys, your dreams won't wait for you and you're never too old (or too young) to chase them. Just remember to be present for what matters most. You're all my world.
- Rush

To Yonitte Hela Kinsella
- Topher

Contents

Tell Us What You Think

Let other readers know what you thought of *Hidden WOMBAT*. Please write an honest review for this book at your favorite online bookstore.

★★★★★

INTRODUCTION

Then one of thy stone upon an hundred fold
After the first and second right fermentation
Of mercury crude turneth it to fine gold.

—Isaac Newton, alchemist, mad as a hatter

We are living in an age of alchemy. Look up "product-market fit," and you'll be deluged with books, interviews, and seminars that promise to help you find it. Everyone promises they have it; no one seems to possess it—like the fabled instructions for transmuting lead into gold. This is evident in product development. The number of teams thrashing around with the same problem suggests the lead-to-gold premise—achieving that hallowed product-market fit—may be wrong from the start.

You've probably heard the claim that 90 percent of start-ups and new products fail. The claim should make your skin crawl. It's wrong. And we all know it's wrong. But we struggle to clarify why.

Why?

Why do intelligent, driven, well-resourced people have slot-machine odds of business success?

This book is our answer to that question. Our goal is to show you that product-market fit is a symptom of a broken innovation process. We will introduce you to the core insight from the Stanford Byers Center for Biodesign—that the reversed market-product fit process guarantees success. We expand this program and tailor its approach to work in any industry. And throughout, we will call out WOMBATs (**w**astes **o**f **m**oney, **b**rains, **a**nd **t**ime) that have bitten us in the past. Because understanding how not to do something is as important as knowing the best practice.

Our goal is to fill the world with better products and superior services. To do that, we must first convince you it's possible. Second, we must give you the plan to do it yourself—what we call needs-driven innovation.

Read this book, and you will be entertained. Follow this book, and you will be successful.

—Rush & Topher

Chapter I

THE INNOVATION PROBLEM

I created a vision of David in my mind and simply carved away every-thing that was not David.

—Michelangelo, being particularly unhelpful

If we'd ever picked up an innovation book that we liked—that really solved our problem—we wouldn't have spent the time to write this one.

Our problem is that we're not artists. Neither of us just follows his gut or gets visited by muses. We're workers. You give us a system—something that makes sense—and we'll run it perfectly. In our best moments, you might call us craftsmen. But no system? Then we're just slapping paint against canvas, and yeah . . . it's not going in the Louvre.

In picking up this book, you've told us something about yourself. You are tasked with creating something new and useful. You are asked to look at the world, see what's missing, and fill that gap. Sounds amazing, but it's horror in practice. You have to deviate from what is established. And that very act will expose you to risk and criticism long before the outcome is known.

First off, thank you. Everything good in the world was built by people like you, deciding to create no matter what. Second off, taking this risk would be a lot easier if there were a practical, repeatable, successful way to do it. That's why you pick up an innovation book at all—for the promise of a system stripped of mystery.

That's not what you get with most innovation books. The vast majority feel like they're written by artists with some magical insight. The book and its spinoff workbooks, courses, seminars, and coaching usually have the following qualities:

1. The expert can describe the results you'll get, but . . .
2. They cannot describe how it works so you get those results without them . . .
3. So you have to hire them.

Unhelpful and off putting.

If you are leading a team trying to invent the future, innovation is more than an alchemy-lite academic exercise—this matters. *You* are going to have to suggest a company initiative. *You* are going to have to assemble and lead a team to reach that goal. *You* are going to be judged on a timeline that will feel far too short and others feel is too long. *You* have to get this right.

Imagine a hunter-gatherer tribe on the savannah. They bring their best bows and sharpest arrows to hunt down wild game. Failure is starvation—for themselves and all their kin. The hunters see a gazelle, sneak within bow range, and loose their arrows. Animal hit. Thud. Families fed. The tribe celebrates with bonfires, folklore, and fanfare. The hunters are heroes.

That's the sales team. They know their target, have done this before, and can hit their quota on a quarterly, biannual, or annual cadence. Not easy; not impossible. But in product development, you're tasked with more. Somewhere out there is an elephant. No one has ever seen one, but they heard from another hunter that they're big and can feed the tribe for a month. Now get one!

So how do you hunt an elephant? How do you recognize it? What tools bring it down? How do you look the village elder in the eye and say, "Yes, I can get you one of those this season"? Not only do you not know where to begin; you can't tell a good hunting strategy from a bad one until the season is over. If you fail, everyone starves. And your reward for succeeding? Somewhere out there is a unicorn. No one has ever seen one . . .

That is the expectation placed on innovation leaders in growing, stable, and mature companies.

Good luck.

For large companies and small start-ups alike, the risk of losing the hunt is too high to waste time using the wrong tools. And if you're responsible for innovation, you're probably scrambling toward any you can find that look like they might help.

Credit where due: there are some good methods out there. Agile. Lean Start-up. Design Thinking. Six Sigma. Jobs to Be Done. We've taken some great lessons from these authors, but in the end, to us, these feel like pieces of what we're looking for. They are ornaments, but we're still missing the tree, the structure on which each hangs, the system that makes it make sense.

Some good news? We found it. The tool to pierce that thick hide of this-better-work innovation was forged in the hell that is medical technology. And that's the very reason it could not have come from anywhere else. Here's why.

If you're trying to bring a product to market for just anyone—say, an app on your phone—you don't need to get it right the first time. You can just A/B test it, deploy it to thousands or millions of people, and sift the data later to figure out what worked and what didn't. If your product crashes in beta, who cares? This is all the normal journey of pivoting to find product-market fit.

If you bring that kind of lazy, slapdash thinking into medicine, you just killed a patient. In medicine, the stakes are insane. The costs are insane. The regulatory hurdles are insane. You cannot bet on losers. You have to get religion around your customer, the market, all the stakeholders, and every previously failed product before you even dream about trying it on a patient. How's that for stakes? How would *you* innovate in that environment?

The biodesign process is the result of what can survive, even thrive, in that hellscape. It puts the patient at the center of all decisions, creates a system around their unmet needs, and treats every step of development with an exactness that leaves no room for waste. It is market-product fit, not the reverse. It is the cleanest, clearest system for innovating in an environment where risks must be purged, costs must be contained, and results must be meaningful. It is done with the same care you might use when defusing a bomb. Sound like your situation?

The Stanford Biodesign Innovation Fellowship is how this is currently taught to healthcare innovators. It is specifically designed to take in engineers, MDs, and MBAs and over the course of a year spit out entrepreneurs who will build the medical companies of the future. In its first twenty years, it has been responsible for:

- 10 million people helped with technologies invented during Biodesign training at Stanford.
- 56 health technology companies launched based on needs found during the program[1]
- 68 additional health tech companies founded beyond fellowship training[2]
- $2 billion in funding raised during and after the program by fellows[3]
- 2,600-plus full-time employees in companies launched during and after[4]

It's important to point out that this was accomplished by a program only twenty years young within a cohort of two hundred graduates. It's shocking because all this has come from so few. Imagine the world if ten to one hundred times as many people could learn it. Most of those who are tasked with changing the world aren't free to spend a year in Palo Alto. They are almost everywhere else, from start-ups to Fortune 500s. To change the world, the world-changing system needs to reach you.

You need the system that was formed under incredible stress and tested against impossible standards, and you need it in a form that can

---

1 - "News and Events," Stanford Byers Center for Biodesign, https://biodesign.stanford.edu/news---events.html.

2 - "Trainee Outcomes," Stanford Byers Center for Biodesign, https://biodesign.stanford.edu/our-impact/trainee-outcomes.html.

3 - Ibid.

4 - Ibid.

work for you, your team, and your industry today. You need a system that works anywhere—outside academia, outside medicine, and outside Silicon Valley. That's what we've written for you (and for ourselves).

With this book, we've taken the biodesign system, drawn out the core principles, augmented them to work in any field, and tailored them to fit the corporate environment. Untethered from medicine, biodesign is best thought of as needs-driven innovation (NDI). There are four stages to NDI, each with its own goals, processes, and pitfalls:

1. Inquire: Build an innovation team and give them clear boundaries.
2. Identify: Find important, unmet, measurable marketplace needs.
3. Invent: Create and vet solutions for the most profitable needs.
4. Implement: Remove product risk before going to market.

We've also paired NDI with the most powerful teacher there is—the failures of others. Throughout this book, we discuss the cardinal sin of innovation: WOMBAT. It stands for a waste of money, brains, and time. It's what you can never do but is rarely obvious. Here are some examples.

WOMBAT 1: There are more than 600,000 Americans with kidney failure. If they don't go to a dialysis center three times per week or get a transplant, they die. So they spend about fifteen hours a week at a dialysis center. There's a company working on a faster machine that could speed up dialysis by thirty minutes per session. With average reimbursements of about $2 per minute, that would save $60 on every patient every session—$5.6 billion per year of time could be saved if everyone used it! The technology worked, but the business failed. Why?

WOMBAT 2: There are about 20 million breathing tubes used each year during medical procedures and in the intensive care unit. The problem with being on a ventilator is every twenty-four hours, your risk of getting pneumonia increases—and pneumonia kills. A company has the brilliant idea of coating the tube with an antibacterial agent. They spend tens of millions of dollars developing and testing the product—ending with a seven-hundred-patient study in *The Journal of the American Medical Association*, proving their tube dramatically reduces the rate of pneumonia. Compared to the regular $2 plain tubes, this new coated tube would be worth over $300 given all the pneumonias it prevents. The technology worked, but this business, too, failed. Why?

WOMBAT 3: A friend has to stay within fifty feet of a bathroom at all times because of bladder spasm; otherwise, she risks being incontinent. A company develops a drug that is injected into the bladder muscles to relax them, reducing spasm and giving her time to get to the bathroom when she wants to. It works—80 percent of patients experience a cure. For the other 20 percent, it's too effective, and they can no longer pee. These patients then require a catheter to drain their bladder until the effects of the drug wear off in a few months. Despite the 80/20 benefit, fewer than 10 percent of eligible patients try it. Why?

It turns out that time isn't always money, narrow problems don't support broad solutions, and the presence of a complication can be more painful than the absence of a benefit. Someone had to learn these lessons painfully, but that someone doesn't have to be you.

Maybe those teams didn't see those problems ahead of time. Worse, maybe they did, but the pressure placed on them to deliver took away their options. What choices do you have if you only have one way to win? Risks be damned, you have to get to market and hope for the best. Needs-driven innovation gets teams out of the uncomfortable position of having one egg in one basket. With NDI, you have so many ways to win that you cannot fail—every experiment that doesn't work or prototype that the user hates is just one more mistake you didn't make later. With this system in place, you also have the confidence to spot something that violates it—to call a WOMBAT a WOMBAT—and save your company a great deal of regret. By learning what you should do (NDI) and what you shouldn't do (chase WOMBATs), you'll be able to innovate in any field, at any time, with any number of constraints, repeatedly.

How's that for an innovation book?

People have been fooled into thinking they understand expertise. They think being an expert is knowing all the right things. An expert is defined not by what they know, but by what they say no to. The expert gardener knows where to prune, the expert hunter knows when to stay still and what shots to let pass, and the expert surgeon knows when not to operate. That's what makes studying the world of medicine so shocking: you can see in practice what was learned painfully (and at others' expense). It's the high stakes that force this system into existence, and it's a system that we apply to give you a surgical understanding of innovation.

In innovation, as in surgery, it takes lots of exposure and repetition to develop expertise. We've been in the fortunate position of participating in thousands of innovation cycles, from the largest medtech companies in the world to the most cutting-edge start-ups in stealth mode. We've seen what went wrong and have used needs-driven innovation to spot and eliminate WOMBATs before research and development (R&D) gets underway. We will share these lessons with you while hiding identities (the most painful failures tend to be the most valuable.) Throughout, this will be presented in a direct, no-nonsense style typical of a surgeon or CEO. You're busy, and we're not here to WOMBAT.

A quick note before our bios: Throughout this book, we will use "we" to indicate insights shared by us both—Rush and Topher. Where personal anecdotes involve only one of us, we will indicate to whom the story, opinion, or experience belongs. Our introductions are one such place.

About Rush

As Stanford Biodesign's associate director of corporate education, I have trained five thousand-plus people from top medtech companies since 2015. As an innovation strategy consultant, I have consulted with more than a dozen Fortune 500 medtech firms on several multibillion-dollar global product franchises. Beyond these pursuits, I also serve as a strategy advisor, seed investor, and board member for several venture-backed start-ups. Previously, I worked in operational roles at small companies as CEO, COO, and chief product officer, ranging from the first napkin sketch to more than $150 million in revenue. I've been an executive in residence at the University of Texas, where I founded the Texas Biodesign Program with MD Anderson, and I have been a prolific inventor, with one hundred-plus pending or issued patents. In my entrepreneurial career, I've launched five start-ups—one failure, two successful exits, one in stealth, and my latest venture-backed company, Vynca Health, which has already helped over a million patients.

About Topher

I (Topher) was studying for an important medical school exam and noticed that this widely used book had some mistakes. Inside the book cover, a ten-dollar bounty was offered for any errors found. I've always liked writing and I needed the money, so I published a website that cataloged and corrected every mistake so anyone studying had the best information. Five hundred errors later, I was hired to edit and author future editions. Skipping forward, I did well on that test and became a trauma surgeon with an interest in elaborate Halloween costumes. I combined these skills and launched a trauma mannequin company out of my garage. This went OK. I went to Stanford Biodesign so that my next company would go better. While there, I spent time screening hundreds of companies for an investment group and learned the differences between good and great. I also consulted for Fortune 500 companies on how to bring biodesign-like innovation internally. Forever combining unrelated things, I used lessons from investing and surgery to make it work. Using this hybrid system, I cofounded Watershed Therapeutics and serve as CEO.

Frequently Asked Questions

When we brief CEOs and other corporate leaders on needs-driven innovation, we hear the same or similar questions in response. You may have some of those questions yourself. So now that we've established the *why* of NDI, and before the *how*, let's answer the *what* of NDI.

Does This Book Teach Biodesign?

No. This book is written beyond the scope of medical technologies. So we will not be discussing, for example, regulatory compliance and FDA approval. That's what the original biodesign textbook, *Biodesign: The Process of Innovating Medical Technologies*, does.[5] Biodesign is laser-fo-

---

5 - Yock et all. 2015. *Biodesign: The Process of Innovating Medical Technologies*. 2nd ed. Cambridge University Press.

cused on medical technology innovation while teaching students what they need to know to become innovators; Biodesign is not a guide for the corporate ecosystem.

If you came to this book because you care about life sciences, everything you learn here complements Biodesign. If you're not in medtech, this book is your fast pass to a comprehensive understanding of what matters when applying Needs-Driven Innovation in any industry.

Does This Work in Companies?

Yes. Adoption of the needs-driven biodesign approach began at major medical technology companies in 2013. Since then, Abbott, Baxter, Becton Dickinson, Dexcom, Edwards Lifesciences, Johnson & Johnson, Stryker, Teleflex, Zimmer Biomet, and many others are at various stages of adoption, up to full incorporation into their company-wide innovation playbooks. The earliest and most complete adopters have used those insights to launch multiple products with strategically important intellectual property and act with confidence on a few hundred million and multibillion-dollar acquisitions. Most importantly, the teams now speak a common innovation language that makes it more efficient and repeatable to avoid WOMBAT, maximizing the value of their innovation pipeline while spending resources on fewer projects overall.

It took us a long time and a lot of pain to figure out how to achieve these kinds of results. When we first introduced biodesign to corporate clients, it broke. Everyone's first instinct is to exactly copy Stanford Biodesign's Innovation Fellowship—create a small cross-functional team of high performers siloed away from the business for a year to hunt a unicorn. But there were problems. Teams would waste time trying to write the perfect need statement, and their executive champions didn't know how to judge what a good need statement looked like. Accessing clinical users and patients was almost impossible—blocked by the risk and compliance department. Technical experts had never worked together outside their product-line silos—they usually competed with each other for budget. The teams would work hard for months, only to have their most innovative product killed by a single department manager on the review committee.

Large companies attract amazing talent—people who could have worked anywhere and chose to work where their effort would have the largest impact—so when the system doesn't work for them, the blame rests on the teaching. So we got to work.

We've spent more than a decade learning how to implement NDI in the corporate environment, working with companies across hundreds of engagements in North America, Europe, and Asia. We know what doesn't work, and when you give talented people the benefit of seeing around corners, it is transformational. We love this work and could do it for decades more, but we realized that we don't scale. We can't do this everywhere ourselves—we need partners to know what we know. We need you. Our goal is to help the world eliminate WOMBAT. We need the world to know the methodology that helps identify it. That's why we wrote this book.

Isn't NDI Just the Process of Elimination?

Experts approach a problem the way sculptors approach stone—get rid of the blocks that don't belong so you can get to work on what is rough now but deserves a smooth finish. This approach is reflected in the tools of their trade. No one starts with sanding paper—they start with a hammer and a spike.

Needs-driven innovation is the chisel, sanding, and perfect polish. After the fact, a product that has gone through NDI will be called "obvious" because it fits the market's needs perfectly. But chisels come first. Clearing WOMBATs is the brutal work of the chisel. Better early and definitive so your teams spend their efforts where they matter.

These methods can be followed step by step. The reasons for them are clear enough that you will remember them without having to memorize them. They will turn you into an artisan.

Chapter 2

YOU HAVE IT BACKWARD

A step backward, after making a wrong turn, is a step in the right direction.

—Kurt Vonnegut, explaining a pivot

My (Rush) first experience with innovation was founding a drug delivery start-up called LyoGo. We started out interviewing diabetics, and several told us about a time when they passed out from hypoglycemia (low blood sugar). These episodes required paramedics to rush to the scene and rapidly administer intravenous medication. This was scary and expensive. So our idea was simple—why can't diabetics have an emergency injector the way people with allergies have an EpiPen? So we built it. After winning tons of awards, earning a feature in *Fortune* magazine, raising a series A from investors, and working with some of the most amazing NGOs and pharmaceutical companies in the world, the technology worked—but the company failed.

Dejected but persistent, I entered the Biodesign Innovation Fellowship. Curious, I inserted the description for LyoGo into the regular biodesign process to understand where it went wrong, a necessary postmortem. My partner and I ended up finding more than two hundred need statements—each a one-sentence business plan—and we went through the process of sorting them out, slowly filtering out the worst.

I was humiliated. LyoGo didn't crack the top forty opportunities. My first start-up—the one I had spent six years of my life on—turned out to be far from amazing. The exercise revealed it to be more akin to a "Hey, wouldn't it be cool if . . .?" type of idea that gets people excited but not activated—that's why it failed. Had I followed the biodesign process, I would have avoided all the pain of six years of wasted time and money. To make it starker, there were forty other ideas that would have had a bigger impact on the world and would have been even easier to pull off. I fell for a WOMBAT.

To reverse the usual innovation process that churns out product-first, market-later failures, we're going to begin our WOMBAT-slaying efforts in an unusual place: language. We've found that if we can't agree on basic definitions—such as what is a need or a solution or a stakeholder—then all else is in vain.

The Language of Needs-Driven Innovation

When we present NDI at on-site workshops, we often find ourselves redefining terms because when we talk about needs and the client's team talks about needs, we're not even talking about the same phenomenon. Everything downstream from that moment in the conversation is a waste of time. So let's make the following promise to each other: we are all going to know what we are talking about when we talk about it.

The first person we care about is the **anchor beneficiary**, or *anchor* for short. We care about the anchor beneficiary because their *need* is what makes the world turn. What is a need? A **need** arises when something essential for survival, well-being, or fulfillment is lacking for the anchor.

In every industry, there is an anchor beneficiary. Some even have a specific name for this person. In medicine, the anchor is called the patient. In education, the anchor is the student; in journalism, the anchor is the reader; and on and on.

Industry	Common Name of the Anchor Beneficiary
Health care	Patient
Education	Student
Public transportation	Passenger
Retail	Consumer
Financial services	Investor
Mass media & film	Audience
Nonprofit	Beneficiary
Government	Constituent

Without patients, there would be no health-care industry. Without students, there would be no need for teachers or schools or online courses. Without passengers, there would be no transportation industry to move them from point A to point B. Without readers, there would be no need for journalists or authors. If there wasn't a need, there would be no reason for that ecosystem to exist. If you're in industry, you already talk about "user needs," or you talk about "customer needs." These user and customer needs might overlap with those of the anchor, but they don't have to. *The need we're talking about is always about the anchor.*

That's not to say we only care about the anchor beneficiary—far from it. In all cases of a need being met, there are four functional roles that must also be addressed. These roles are the **anchor beneficiary**, the **user**, the **decision-maker**, and the **payer**. Each of these is a **role** played by one or more **stakeholder(s)**. And like the four horsemen of the apocalypse, they declare themselves by their ability to destroy your product or service if what you are doing doesn't work for their **acceptance criteria**. These are the roles that have veto power—don't forget about them or make them angry. Whatever your solution is to the anchor's need, it must address the criteria of all stakeholder roles in the ecosystem, or it's destined to fail.

Early on in the book, our examples are mostly medical. Why? It helps to have the four stakeholder roles clearly separated when first learning about them. Later in the book, once these ideas are cemented, we move to anecdotes in other industries.

You also might be thinking, *What about the customer? Aren't they king?* A customer is what exactly? Who the customer is can change, even for the same product. Different business model, same product, different customer. Take Tylenol: you're the customer when you buy it at the corner drugstore, but you're not if you had a bike accident, and the doctor at the hospital gave you some. The hospital bought it, but the reimbursement for your medical care comes from your insurance. *Customer* is a vague term that brings confusion and argument into innovation. It only means something after you innovate. So for now, let's avoid the word *customer* and stick to the four stakeholder roles.

Let's run through an example so the shared terminology sticks.

As of the writing of this book, my (Topher) two boys still wet the bed. My boys don't care one whit about this, but I do. By the rules of NDI, we anchor the need on the young boys. You could argue that a beneficiary of the need getting solved is the parent, and you wouldn't be wrong. But these arguments go back and forth on teams and eat up a lot of energy, which doesn't help move the project forward, so we decide to always anchor the need on the person or group that, if they didn't have the problem, would obviate the need. That's the bed wetters.

What about the other stakeholder roles? The parents are almost certainly going to be the decision-makers and the payers, but the user might be the boys, the parents, or both. It all depends on what product or service you design, and you don't know that right now—so keep your options open.

When you introduce your new product, it will meet the **population**. The population is not "kids," "kids from three to five years of age," or "boys between four and six years of age." The population is only those people who, when using your product, will have their need met. Why else would they give you their money?

To understand this population, you must uncover the **mechanism** underlying their need that causes it to exist in the first place. In medicine, we call this pathophysiology. For the nocturia example, we must know if it occurs because of diet (too much water, salt, and sugar before bed), sleep patterns (NREM sleep predominates at this age), anatomy (weak urethral sphincters), or some other cause. A solution that limits fluids before bed won't work on kids with deep sleep patterns, a sleep monitor that wakes the kid up during REM sleep might not work on a kid with a weak sphincter, and so on. It's not hard to imagine well-intentioned products failing for lack of understanding the mechanism.

The best business schools in the world push everyone to define the largest market—to make a product that is the most inclusive—but it's a WOMBAT. Narrow problems do not support broad solutions. You need to focus on a **homogeneous population** with a **homogeneous problem** if you want to ensure success. If you don't, your solution will partially work for part of the population, risking total failure.

So let's say you make a product and try to test it. Why would the stakeholders reject it? What criteria are they using to judge it? Back to the bed-wetting example.

It turns out there are lots of products for parents trying to meet the needs of leaky boys. One is a pad that goes under the kids and vibrates them awake if it detects moisture. My boys sleep right through it, so now I have wet sheets and a wet device to clean. Another is a pee-jama that replaces diapers (saving me money) but requires I wash it every morning or buy a whole bunch of them. Just swapping one type of laundry for another makes me feel cheated. While it keeps the bed dry, it isn't getting my son trained to stay dry. I abandon them both and go back to pull-ups. Why?

The criteria for the solution are being revealed. The product has to keep the bed dry *and* not require more work from me or my wife. If it doesn't meet these criteria, we will not use it. A product that also moves my kids toward independence would make me choose product A over product B. These are things I can consider only if the more important criteria are met first.

We've also discovered how I will **value** the solution—by the money I save by not buying diapers anymore. This is the economically important outcome that will determine how much money I am willing to spend on a solution.

And how did we learn this was a problem at all? You could argue we wrote this entire chapter just to complain about it. That's a strong **signal of unmetness**. Signals of unmetness show us that the anchor has a problem. When that signal goes away, we know our solution works. Additional signals could be tied to economic value, such as pull-up spend or laundry costs.

A signal of unmetness can point to an economically important **outcome** that would be created when the action taken on the problem is successful. For example, the boys' sleeping through the night without bed-wetting would reduce the amount spent on diapers. There are many signals of unmetness: parental frustration, more frequent sheet washing than desired, and so on. But the outcome as we define it is the key value proposition that, if achieved, would get your decision-maker to say yes, your payer to pay, your user to use, and your anchor beneficiary to be relieved of their need.

A **need statement** can now be constructed:

1. Need
2. Anchor population
3. Outcome

It reads like this: *a way to keep the bed dry at night in four-to-six-year-old boys prone to nocturia to reduce spend on diapers.*

This need statement is a lodestar for the team—it is a one-sentence business plan. It's the simple way to stay focused on what you need to do (action to take on a problem), who you need to do it for (anchor population), and what matters when you do it (valuable outcome). The need statement is our foundation throughout NDI to discover if there is a real market for a product, if the market can be reached, and as a screen for products that delight every stakeholder.

NDI versus Others

Now that we know what we are both talking about when it comes to need, we can delve into a deeper comparison as to why NDI is the most effective, most complete, most versatile way to innovate. In our work with companies, we have faced a lot of questions asking how NDI is different, or why it is better. Often the person asking the question has experience with one or more ways to come up with a new product or service, so let's break them down with the following chart.

	Needs-Driven Innovation	Design Thinking, User-Centered Design	JTBD, Lean Start-up, DTV, Agile	6σ, Lean/Kaizen
First Focus	Anchor stakeholder	User	Customer	Business
Articulation	In the need statement	In the how-might- we or empathy statement	In the job, canvas, or value statement	In the problem statement
Scope	Can change the customer, user, and/or venue to solve the anchor's need	Delight a specific user	Create value for the target customer	Improve an organization's efficiency
Drawbacks	Output may challenge you to disrupt yourself	Heterogeneous users and/or users stuck in a set workflow	Anchored to a specific customer or initial MVP idea	You may optimize a process that will soon become obsolete

The reason NDI is a more durable, timeless method of understanding innovation should leap out at you—**NDI is the only innovation method that cannot be disrupted by a competitor**. By focusing on the anchor stakeholder and becoming obsessive about how the world interacts with their need, you can see around corners. Let's beat this bed-wetting example to death, shall we?

A diaper company hires three innovation teams to help them address this market. They recognize their customers have this problem and want to take advantage of owning the customer funnel. They hire a design-thinking team, a jobs-to-be-done team, and a needs-driven innovation team.

The design-thinking team looks at bed-wetting and asks, "How might we make staying dry at night cool?" They become obsessed with engagement from the young boys. Through the miracle of hypercolor technology, they make diapers that have dinosaurs and robots on them that, when they get wet, disappear. The boys learn that keeping themselves dry means the cool design stays in the morning, and so they strive for it. For some kids it works, but it adds some extra cost for a cost-conscious consumer.

A jobs-to-be-done team looks at the problem and designs a monitor that can be placed in the diaper to track what time each boy wets the bed each night for a week (define, prepare). It then switches over to an alarm clock function that wakes them up ten minutes early to go to the bathroom (execute). It slowly expands the interval until the boys make it through the night dry. If there is ever a breakthrough event, the system resets the schedule (monitor, modify). They boast that no system works faster to bed train, and they are correct (conclude). It's expensive, but it works wonders for some kids.

The NDI team comes back with something different—make the diaper *less* absorbent. A need criteria they identified for the child was to absorb at most two bed-wetting episodes per night to keep their sheets dry. Years ago, the company had a marketing campaign as the most absorbent pull-ups on the market. They had overengineered their pull-ups to absorb 400 percent more liquid than an average kid needed to stay dry through the night. As a result, their cost of goods sold (COGS) was much higher than it needed to be. They were wasting money chasing a claim that wasn't meaningful to solving the need, and the lack of available profit to spend on marketing was a painful drag on their ability to protect their market share.

The CEO was shocked and immediately authorized the R&D team to begin the process of developing a less absorbent pull-up, which ended up being thinner, more discreet, and more comfortable as a bonus. The kids loved it because it was more comfortable, and parents had the same net experience that they have today at a lower price. The company's COGS decreased by 20 percent, and they used part of their higher margins to more aggressively market the new streamlined pull-ups, which increased market share and profitability.

Shocking but yes, this happened. While a few details may be different to retain anonymity, all of the examples in this book are real; made-up stories are WOMBAT.

This is a good time to point out something that might have bothered you—the NDI team didn't help boys and girls get potty trained any faster. They judged it a WOMBAT. Instead, they identified an adjacent opportunity that was more beneficial to the anchor, user, decision-maker, and payer without any negative impact to the user, creating a more comfortable diaper at a lower price.

The key insight that the NDI team had was that there were a lot of different causes of nocturia, and no single product was going to help all kids progress any faster to staying dry at night. Weak sphincter? Too much water before bed? Bad dream? Many heterogeneous (different) causes of a problem make it impossible to solve with a single solution. Instead, you have to find an area where things become homogeneous, and regardless of why they are voiding their bladders, all kids who pee at night send the urine out of their urethra before it hits the sheets. Pull-ups already prevent sheets from getting wet via every mechanism of bed-wetting. Importantly, this is also a problem that self-resolves as the child ages, and, although frustrating, nobody dies. You just have to wait long enough, and the problem goes away.

That doesn't mean we can't have some fun—and we did in writing this book. So just for kicks, we asked ourselves, "How might we make holding urine fun?" Our hypothetical prototype goes underneath the toilet seat and presents a target like "whack-a-wombat." The boys aim at the target, and after their stream hits it, it makes an *ack* sound and retracts under the bowl, hides for three seconds, and then timidly reappears. It does this over and over. The boys find this hysterical and start learning to urinate, hold their stream, urinate, hold their stream, over and over to make it scream more. Without knowing it, without the parents having to do anything, the boys are training their urethral sphincter muscles. Early tests show the boys stay dry within a week, and it's available on our website for a limited time only. WOMBAT.

While comical, there is power in being specific and in understanding the facts surrounding your need. This should have led you to the conclusion that the value of this need isn't significant. For each month saved, it's just the cost of a pack of pull-ups. Maybe. You want to "get religion" around understanding if your **unmet need** is linked to an **unmet market**.

When Backward Is Forward

If you're going to bring a product to market, here's what you cannot escape: you have to know the market, you have to make a product that works for the market, and the market has to be valuable enough to sustain a repeatable business model. Otherwise, the music stops. This seems obvious to the point of insulting, but just look at what happens if you don't keep it stupid and simple.

While not the same as shared language, shared understanding of this fundamental knowledge—what it means to know a market and make a product for it—is as critical to eventual success. Let this be a reference for all innovators from now till the end of time.

An Unmet Market

Unmet market is our term for a group of people who all share the same unmet need. Crucially, they all have the same version of this unmet need such that a single product could address them all. In practice, this gets built up from an initial observation, and this is what that looks like.

Someone

Anecdotes are what new markets look like in the beginning. We *love* anecdotes. But if you can't find someone in the world with this need and physically meet it, the need is not real. This strict filter up front prevents "wouldn't it be cool if" ideas generated by the team from entering the process.

Many Someones

One person with a need is a start, but multitudes are needed for a business. You need a bottom-up signal that many people with this need are not hard to find.

The Same Way

All the someones must have the need in the same way. What does this mean? "I don't like my blender" might sound like a need, but one person wants a replacement that is quieter, and the other wants a blender that is powerful enough to liquify an avocado with the pit. Skipping over why anyone would blend an entire avocado, do you think the same product improvement will satisfy both people? This point gets missed as it gets more subtle, and in short order, a market your staff told you was $4 billion dwindles to $40 million on product launch. Remember, the need is the thing that must be accomplished to relieve the anchor beneficiary of their problem. Narrow problems don't support broad solutions because the mechanism of action that creates the problem can differ from person to person. So either make a quieter blender or an industrial one, but don't think you can sell the same product to both markets and simultaneously fend off more specialized competitors.

A Commercial Path

There exists a stakeholder who will give you enough money for your product to justify building and selling it.

Just because you calculate the value of solving the need at $1 billion doesn't mean there is anyone with $1 billion to give you. Take migraines, for example. The patient hates them and can't buy their way out of them but, on average, has maybe $200 a month to spend on the problem. The pain isn't fixed, and they miss work; you calculate the economic impact at $400 a month per person per year.

If you come up with a solution that the patient has to pay for, it has to be under $200 a month. If you come up with a solution that the employer elects to pay for, you can charge $400 a month. In no scenario do you get to recoup the total value of the $200 per month and the $400 per month because no single person bears both costs.

Happiness

All things being equal, it would be best if the stakeholders involved in the need were all happy your product existed. Anger downstream from a different stakeholder requires happiness upstream for the anchor, so make sure if someone is unhappy, they're too late to matter.

Here's a famous example from cardiology. Cardiac surgeons have performed open-heart surgery for decades. Then endovascular solutions became available, allowing repair of arteries from inside the vessel, leading to fewer big surgeries. Surgeons weren't interested as they thought their skillset worked just fine, and this new technology was unproven. They continued with what they knew.

Cardiologists, on the other hand, had no way to fix hearts except through this new endovascular technique. So cardiologists started using this product and generated incredible amounts of revenue for themselves at the expense of cardiac surgeons. Cardiac surgeons hated this and fought hard. Who won that war—and why?

When people develop heart disease, they get referred to cardiologists—not to cardiac surgeons. It's only after the cardiologist runs out of treatments that they are referred to the cardiac surgeon. Now, the cardiologist doesn't have to refer as many patients to the surgeon because of these new tools. The cardiac surgeons can scream all they want, but if they are downstream from the decision, they are downstream from control of the market.

If you're going to disrupt a market, the upstream stakeholder has to be thrilled, and the downstream stakeholder has to have no way to stop it.

Awareness

You must be able to identify who has the need, and they must know they have that need.

Some needs you don't know you have. For example, the *feijoa* is an incredibly tasty fruit of South America—its flavor is like the best notes of strawberry, pineapple, and guava combined. You might crave it, but you don't know you do because you've never tasted it. By our calculations, some people should be customers for our *feijoa* business, theoretically, but if zero percent of them know what a *feijoa* tastes like, we have no actual market unless we spend an enormous amount of money to give everyone a taste.

Reachable

The people who know they have the need must be concentrated through a funnel and reachable through a channel.

If you have a solution for colon cancer but the people with colon cancer are evenly distributed throughout the country, how are you going to get to them? If everyone with the diagnosis is referred to a colon care specialty center, then life becomes easier—you can launch your product in these areas of concentrated patients. But if there is no funnel to concentrate them into an accessible sales channel, you will have to mass market. Since only 0.03 percent of Americans receive a colon cancer diagnosis each year, a Super Bowl commercial to market a treatment would be a waste of money. And if your product doesn't work in the hands of your average Walmart shopper, a retail market will kill it. It's important to know this before you design the solution

That's the market. Now, the product itself.

Market-Product Fit, Not Product-Market Fit

What do many innovators do instead of everything discussed in this section so far? They see an anecdote from the market; say, "Wouldn't it be cool if . . .?"; jump straight to prototyping the idea; and then try to implement it. Insane. An even worse version of this mistake is "Our competitor just launched this, so we are already behind and need to move fast to catch up." Product life cycles from the initial idea to market launch are two to ten-plus years, depending on the industry.

If your innovation strategy is based on benchmarking yourself to competition, you will always be years behind the leading competitor. And you don't even know if the competitor is right. Why make an assumption they're smarter or know more than you? NDI gives you the confidence to spot when a new product brought to market by a competitor is wrong.

It should be obvious that deeply understanding the market, while maybe not fun and sexy to most, is where all the insights to your new product are. Once you know the market, your product cannot help but become perfectly tailored to it. This is why market-product fit, not product-market fit, is the way to go. If you lead with a product, you are in the almost-hopeless position of finding a market that just happens to match it. Hence pivot, pivot, pivot—what a WOMBAT.

The bigger the organization, the more important this is to get right. In especially large companies with an existing innovation process, the teams never deliver quite enough innovation. These companies have a process for vetting an idea, testing prototypes, and producing a well-thought-out business plan, but their biggest flaw is that each product development team only works on a few ideas at a time. Typically, an executive or key opinion leader will throw an idea over the fence to the innovation team. That team will vigorously chase down that idea, and, because it came from an important person, there is zero political incentive to call their idea a WOMBAT. As a result, projects end up being well thought through yet deliver only mediocre returns because the initial seed was a product idea instead of a need for an entire market.

This is the one-egg-in-one-basket phenomenon, and if the team thinks they only have one chance to succeed, then it's no surprise when they'll back even a rotten egg.

In this type of company, the antidote is a full field of many competitive ideas, all managed by the team, with each idea testing and clearing the same criteria. This keeps the team honest, preventing "favorites" from making it past an important filter. Dispassionate competition ensures not just that the best opportunities are brought forward, but that no weak ideas are allowed to survive—especially if they came from an important person.

Maybe everything here is old hat to you, maybe not. But the next kicker is this: if you are evaluating a number of different markets to enter and you have ten-plus different dimensions by which you evaluate each opportunity, what system are you using to accomplish that? How do you compare watermelons and *feijoas* as you would apples to apples? How do you generate ideas that give you multiple ways to win? And given that the electrical engineer is going to believe in the solution that uses their skills and the mechanical engineer will believe in theirs, how will you objectively screen and choose in a way that everyone accepts and gets you the best product for that market?

Filters and Ranks

Filters and ranks are core to the Inquire phase but are so important we must introduce them here. Filtering and ranking are essential to avoiding WOMBAT. You've heard "measure twice, cut once"? This is the opposite: cut twice, measure once. Why? Because when you have lots of ideas, cutting is cheap while measuring is expensive. Here's how we do it.

Establish your filters. Filters are unflinching. They are applied as a yes or no and never a maybe. This is how decision-makers cull options from a large list down to the ones that are the best and most viable. A filter is simply a criteria by which to make a binary decision. If the filter decision is no, all the other details don't matter.

There are two important things for every filter. First, the person who created it has a rationale that is not dogmatic—you can describe the new information that, if available, would make you revise the filter. The second is that it is applied as early as possible to prevent wasting money, brains, and time on ideas that will never work.

Here's an example. Suppose a homeowner insists that we not use wood for their fence because it rots over time. What if we found a wood that doesn't rot? Would they then be open to a wood fence? Sure. Binary decision, clear rationale, openness to change if new information emerges. The filter is it can't rot—not that it can't be wood.

Ranks are those variables that, after filters are cleared, help you decide which remaining options are best. Ranks are applied second because the depth of understanding required to apply them can be enormous. Ranking is mentally taxing—more than simply making a yes or no judgment. Don't waste energy on ranking opportunities that would have been filtered out.

Note that filters and ranks cannot change because you don't like the results they produce. The danger is that someone's favorite market or idea is *just* outside a filter or rank, but they love it so much, they are willing to bend the rules to let it pass. This should never be done. This destroys teams by destroying the guardrails of the process and places an emotional success ("I get to keep my favorite") over a commercial success ("I want what is going to work best").

Early use of filters and ranks is also an excellent way to achieve stakeholder buy-in. You ask stakeholders to give you criteria for how they would judge a winning idea rather than asking them to evaluate the ideas themselves. Then, only after those criteria are clearly defined, the ideas are judged against them. If the idea succeeds when it's evaluated by the conditions of the criteria, you win; the stakeholders will gladly buy in. We are always surprised by how teams make excuses to keep an idea alive even when they know it fails their filters. The earlier you are honest and brutal with the filters, the better.

This way of thinking permeates the four stages of NDI. Now that this foundational understanding is laid, we head there next, beginning with stage one, Inquire.

Chapter 3

INQUIRE: GET EVERYONE AT THE TABLE

It must be remembered that there is nothing more difficult to plan, more doubtful of success, nor more dangerous to manage than a new system.

—Niccolò Machiavelli, playing it safe

One Champion Is Not Enough

COVID-19 killed 6.8 million people. We could have helped millions of them. The technology was there. Sadly, needs-driven innovation was not.

I (Rush) am on my fifth company at the time of this writing. My second company designed a product for ventilated patients. When you are on a ventilator, having a breathing tube is like having a snorkel shoved down your throat. As an understatement, it is deeply uncomfortable. Without sedating drugs, you would fight like mad to remove it. The trade-off is that those same sedating drugs, by putting you to sleep, don't allow you to move and maintain the health of your muscles, including the muscles you use to breathe.

The idea behind our product was simple enough—numbing the throat will make you more comfortable, you will require less sedation, and you will be able to move and protect your strength. Taken together, these reduce several unwanted side effects such as heart complications, pressure ulcers, and even delirium, which can make patients go crazy and have long-lasting impacts, especially for the elderly.

The product we designed sprayed lidocaine, a dental anesthetic, continuously into the throat, numbing the gag reflex. This drug application was already in use manually for bronchoscopies and upper-GI endoscopies, in which a small camera travels a similar path. The drug was proven to work dramatically—all we had to do was make it automatic.

Great innovation, right? We sold this company to BigCo Inc. in 2015 and waited for it to hit the market. We figured it should have taken twenty-four months to develop, but launch never came. Instead, the product was killed internally. Why?

BigCo had acquired our company because they were in trouble—the FDA had audited them and found their quality control system deficient. Suddenly, BigCo's R&D team had to be reassigned. Instead of bringing their existing products through development, it was all hands on deck to plug every hole the FDA had spotted. The business still needed to grow, so companies like ours were acquired to feed into the product pipeline until the homegrown R&D efforts could resume.

This was a big strategic move. The head of R&D owned it, and his team followed suit. As sometimes happens, there was an unexpected change of leadership. A new head of R&D was brought in, and their first action was to cut everything and start from scratch. They didn't want to be judged based on these legacy ideas—especially the externally acquired ones.

Now, you may be appalled by that story. We were crushed. We had a product that worked in theory, that worked in practice, that physicians wanted, that would save hospitals money, and that would help patients. And here's where it gets sad: In 2020, this product could have helped millions of people on ICU ventilators because it would have allowed patients to have less sedation and a faster recovery. If this tool had been developed and made available, drug and ventilator shortages could have been drastically reduced.

So before we start pouring ourselves into improving the world, let's make sure we know how those solutions will travel through an organization, how they will be judged, and how to make sure that the entire organization—not just one passionate leader—owns and supports the effort.

Titles Do Not Equal Power

I (Topher) joined a Fortune 500 company to lead an innovation team given free rein to create and design solutions in the hospital. The team found several unmet needs attached to large markets. They presented their work to leadership and were given the green light to continue. A total of four months into the effort, they returned with sophisticated product ideas to address each of these needs, any one of which could have been a great new business. A full meeting of leadership was scheduled and the results presented.

"How am I supposed to sell that?"

There was silence. It wasn't just the innovation team who was stunned; it was the rest of the department heads. The head of R&D answered, "This would be sold to ICU physicians. They are the users for this need."

"Yeah? Well, that's not our call point. Our sales team works on commission and quotas. Am I supposed to tell them to make less money while we figure this out? No one is doing that."

And that killed it.

As wild as it sounds, the director of sales was effectively in charge of all innovation. And he didn't even know it. No one in the organization knew it. But this sales director turned out to be a person with the power to say no. And unless someone else had the power to say yes by contracting an outside sales team or changing the compensation structure of the sales force, this wasn't going anywhere. Huge failure of leadership by me.

That's a mistake you make only once.

In this example, the problem was that the filters had been brought in at the wrong stage in the process. That sales director was acting as a filter, but he was invited to chime in at a later stage than he should have been, giving him the power to kill the project even after it had moved far along. The lesson here is that titles do not equal power. Just because the director of sales didn't have a title that implied he had veto power over an R&D project doesn't mean that he didn't have that ability. He did. Power is about both who can say yes and who can say no. And why did he have that power? Because we hadn't defined a "win" beforehand to include opportunities outside the current sales channel—or at least understood what was off limits.

The purpose of the Inquire phase is to account for all key stakeholders in the organization, define the top-down strategic vision, reconcile that with the bottom-up execution of NDI, and prepare the Innovation team to run with the ball.

Inquire Begins from the Top Down

"No" is the key to stopping WOMBAT. Wielded at the right time, it protects the entire organization. At the wrong time, it's a waste. So the first part of any effort must be to define:

1. Every judge of the process in the organization—also called internal stakeholders
2. What corporate goals, if achieved, would all count as a win
3. The criteria (filters and ranks) those judges will use to decide if we met their goals

When to meet? This depends on who sparked the effort.

If the CEO is launching the initiative, then budget is a given, and what we need is alignment with the rest of the executive leadership team (ELT). The CEO can work with the ELT at the next recurring meeting and then gather the judges they propose at their earliest convenience.

If a nonexecutive leader with extra room in their profit and loss (P&L) is launching the effort, they have the budget but will likely need approval to reallocate it in the current fiscal year. They'll need to secure leadership buy-in and subsequent approval from finance. Their best sales pitch is that this year's excess funds can answer a couple of key de-risking questions before a full NDI effort is allocated to next year's budget.

If a nonexecutive leader doesn't have room in their current year's P&L, they have a mountain to climb. The size of that mountain depends on how the company is doing in the current year. If the company is well below bonus targets, great—nobody is getting a bonus anyway, so you might as well invest now for the future. If the company is way above bonus targets, also great—invest the excess in future growth, but watch out for naysayers who will question why you need to do anything different when times are good.

The most challenging spot, where most companies operate, is somewhere in a kind of innovation purgatory—almost or just barely meeting bonus targets. In this middle scenario, it can be challenging to ever get anything truly innovative funded without a complete resetting of expectations at the highest levels of the organization. A slow but steady approach over multiple years with small bits of semisecret funding is usually the best you can do until the opportunity becomes too big for the organization to ignore.

In our experience, a motivated leader needs at least three months to move meaningfully between a first meeting and an approved plan. This is a full-focus, high-touch effort, and teleconference should be a last resort if you want progress. To get buy-in and build a coalition of support, you need face time and lots of trust.

Who joins the coalition? If you're near the top, you have an idea of how things get to you and through what filters they pass. Please let me save you some pain and suggest you ask people at the ground level how they think things move up to you—it will be different.

If you're the big boss, your time is valuable, and everyone knows it, so they'll abstract information before it gets to you, and what abstraction gains in clarity it loses in detail. But detail is what we need. As the person whose political power is driving this effort, you have the responsibility of understanding this up front so the right judges are in the room.

We typically see the following roles around the table as judges:

1. Marketing lead
2. Sales lead
3. R&D lead
4. Strategy/corporate development lead
5. Head of business unit (if the focus of the effort is already known)
6. Anchor stakeholder expert (In health care, this is usually an MD; in the military, an officer; in education, a teacher; etc.)
7. Finance or corporate executive (They'll pick up the tab, so they'd better be in the room.)

Pro tip: Make sure you have at least one pre-meeting with each of these judges one-on-one before the judges' group meeting. The group meeting, like a vote in Congress, should be a formality. The real work of understanding and alleviating concerns to create alignment should be done well before anyone steps foot in the room of the formal meeting.

Define a Win Using Filters

How can we get everyone to agree on what a win looks like and, at the same time, uncover the criteria they will use to judge any outcome? We can do these in parallel with what we lovingly call the piranha method.

If you look at a piranha swimming, you don't learn much about it. If you throw some meat into the water, you'll learn quickly what makes them special.

So throw in some meat. Suggest three or four hypothetical products and their markets to the room. "Which one should we work on?" The point is not to leave the room having chosen one of them for development—that's insane. Instead, listen for why people choose one over the other. What tips the decision? Here are some things you should be listening for:

1. "The market is too small" (revenue targets).
2. "We are a services company, not a product company" (technology first).
3. "Our competitor already has something like that with 80 percent market share" (competitive landscape).
4. "We don't know how to make that" (bias toward current competency).
5. "That's not our call point" (go-to-market strategy).
6. "That would take one or two years of development" (time urgency).
7. "Our customers said this would be cool" (need without verifying market).
8. "Nobody wants that" (criteria assumed based on one person's experience).
9. "Our competitor is entering this space, so we need something too" (fear).
10. "We lost money on a similar project five years ago" (political criteria).
11. "That's a PhD project" (scientific risk).

The first thing you should do with this list is group the items by domain area. Are these corporate, commercial, or development concerns? Make sure that only the people who should be talking about these things are talking about these things.

Once you've determined which group of stakeholders owns that domain, you can ask, "Why is it that you said this? What is the constraint that led to this response?" You are not interested in the conclusion they reached—your interest at this stage is in uncovering their beliefs, biases, and assumptions. The why behind the why.

Looking deeply, you should start to see what the underlying criteria are.

Stakeholder	Commonly Concerns You'll Hear	Underlying Why
Corporate	• We failed at that previously/ No more science projects. • We don't do that kind of product. • Time frame is too long. • Market is too small.	• Fear of repeating a historical embarrassment. • Desire to stay on mission. • Financial pressure for near-term performance. • Meaningful revenue requirements.
Commercial	• We don't have access to that channel, or that's off strategy/We don't have permission to play there. • Too much competition— unless you bring something innovative, it won't sell. • It can't be too expensive, or it won't sell.	• Little experience building a new channel/fear of organizational changes after acquiring that new channel. • Doubts about final product-market fit or timelines from R&D. • Selling on price is easier than selling on value.
Development	• We are really good at making XYZ, but anything outside that won't work. • We have to manage scope creep. • I want to work on something innovative.	• No belief the business will build or buy a new competency. • No faith that the product specification will be correct or that they will be given a reasonable deadline. • They feel the business is too incremental.

On the corporate side, there is concern about history and embarrassment (we failed at that previously), staying on mission (we don't do certain types of products), and getting an early return on the effort (two years is too long) that is sizable (large market).

On the commercial side, concerns about a go-to-market strategy, competition with established products (pro and con), and doubts about product-market fit.

On the development side, concerns about scientific risk (PhD projects are notoriously wandering affairs) and projects being outside current competency. Great! Time to push back.

Remember, NDI is a market-product fit approach. In the beginning of this process, nobody will know enough to know what a good solution looks like. To define the judges' constraints, everyone in the room must "assume invention"—meaning assume there is a black box and that it solves the need. This ensures no one wastes time talking about features, price, etc

Corporate stakeholders come first. If you just sold off a business unit that deals with pulmonology, then it would be off mission to innovate in anything lung related. If you know that revenues need to grow at a 5 percent compound annual growth rate (CAGR), and your current revenues are over $1 billion, then revenue opportunities smaller than $200 million by year four should be uninteresting to you, especially if that market is shrinking. Decisions at the corporate level are the only ones that can open up the marketing and development criteria. If corporate decides you must use an existing sales force for new products, that's critical to know. Similarly, if the organization is willing to acquire a new sales force if the market is big enough, this is also important to uncover—but clarify how big is "big enough."

Calling these "filters" means that these are yes-or-no decisions. Stress test them with probing questions such as "So the organization would say no to a $10 billion revenue opportunity in neurology or any opportunity that takes six years to hit the target revenue?"

We need concrete answers on these kinds of hypotheticals to prevent shiny object syndrome when a good but off-target opportunity shows up later.

The corporate filters might look like this:

1. Markets growing at 6 percent CAGR or greater
2. Markets with fourth-year revenue projections greater than $200 million
3. Aligned with the current mission of cardiovascular disease

Repeat this process with the commercial and development stakeholders.

Examples of commercial filters include:

1. Can be reached with the existing sales force
2. Does not require long training cycles for users
3. Does not interrupt current Q24m cadence of iterative product improvements

Examples of development filters include:

1. Within structural heart cardiovascular disease
2. Devices only (that is, no pharmaceutical approaches)
3. FDA approval pathway the same as something we have done before

It is critical to understand why these criteria are suggested and what that means for the incentive structure and resource constraints of your organization. Every constraint is a narrowing of options. If your options are too narrow, challenge the constraints at this stage.

Are you willing to hire new talent that can unlock a new sales channel? Acquire a new technical competency? Change strategy at the corporate level? If you have short-term incentive structures, are you able to change them to support a two- to three-year effort? Can you effectively message to your board and the public markets that the short-term pain is worthwhile in the long run? Corporate, commercial, and development must have alignment, and that may require corporate to change how people are resourced and rewarded.

You might be tempted to skip involving the development team in this early stakeholder meeting, but that would be a mistake. Till now, their contact with the market has been abstracted through design specs developed by others. Many of them haven't met the anchor. When they design something, they don't see their work post market—a blind spot just as big as the opportunity for an organization that fixes it.

So loop in the dev team at the beginning so they understand the corporate and commercial criteria. Do not worry that the dev team will have a long list of solution constraints because there is nothing to solve at this stage. This is an opportunity to educate the dev team—they need to know we're not solving problems right now; we're finding them. This shared alignment is our focus. We want a strong partnership between development, commercial, and corporate stakeholders, so get everyone aligned toward the same targets and working at the same cadence.

Look at the criteria you've identified so far. Is there enough room for a win-win scenario to emerge? An over-constrained effort will have a long list of filters from corporate, commercial, and development stakeholders. Too many constraints make it harder to find a way to win. Applying the wrong kind of constraints at the wrong part of the process will kill your creativity. The responsibility rests with the corporate stakeholders to either abandon the effort before it starts or modify (or remove) constraints.

Score a Win Using Ranks

Chances are, when defining filters, there will be some waffling, even with the best of teams. Good. That means that these aren't filters—they're ranks.

A rank is not a yes-or-no decision point but a variable you consider in context.

You may have a filter criteria of "more than $100 million additional annual revenue." All opportunities that pass that filter are ranked by how much above $100 million they could achieve. These ranking criteria are stage specific, so we use different measures in the Identify phase than in the Invent phase. The NDI team will dive into the details of their use, but for quick reference, here are a few we commonly use.

Identify— Need Ranks	Description	Ideal vs. Least Ideal State
Market pull	How badly does the market want a solution?	Life-or-death vs. self-resolving problems
Understanding of mechanism	How well do you understand the problem? Is it a new problem with little research?	Well-understood problem vs. science project

Ability to prove success	How costly is it, and how much time is required to prove you met the outcome?	Self-evident vs. multiyear study
Awareness of the problem	Do the stakeholders all know the magnitude of the problem and think it is important?	Everyone aware of this urgent need vs. little awareness
Economic value of the need	(Cost of the problem) x (# in the anchor population with the problem) x (% reduction of the problem based on the outcome)	Highest total value above the filter criteria

A table of common ranks for Invent:

Invent Concept Ranks	Description	Ideal vs. Least Ideal State
Stakeholder criteria	How well does your solution satisfy the criteria from all stakeholders?	All rank criteria met or exceeded vs. only the filter criteria are met
Competitive differentiation	How much better is the solution than others?	Monopoly vs. commodity
Financial constraints	Does the solution fit within the financial criteria defined by the value proposition?	High value, high margin vs. low value, low margin
Execution window	Can you get to market before the market's criteria change?	Quick to market vs. slow to market
Laws and regulations	How easy would it be to get and keep a legally defensible advantage?	Legal and regulatory change unlikely disrupt you vs. high risk of regulation disruption
Company infrastructure fit	How well does it fit within house technical and commercial expertise?	Very close to something you make and sell already vs. completely new to company

Each rank should only be applied in the stage of the process where it is designated. This allows you and your team to separately evaluate all the variables that define what a good need looks like and all the variables that define what a good solution looks like. Trying to do both of those steps at the same time leads to pivot, pivot, pivot, WOMBAT.

The good news is that there are themes within these filters that build on each other from Identify to Invent. How well do you understand the mechanism of action of the problem? Well, that's a technology-free way to understand downstream technical feasibility. How much economic value is created by solving the need? Well, that is a technology-free way to understand potential market size that a specific solution may carve out. By applying the need-level ranks, you are also de-risking your solution-level ranks—just don't ask the wrong question at the wrong time.

Guys, why did you make me read that? I'm not going to be on the NDI team, and this seems like a crazy level of detail. Good question!

To highlight this as a key difference with how biodesign is applied in an academic setting compared to NDI applied in corporations. In an academic setting, the team of students is their own authority of what they want to work on, so biodesign asks the team to set their own filter criteria in the Identify phase. In a corporate setting, letting the team define their own scorecard without leadership's direction would be insane. The judges need to define it with the NDI leader (that's you), ideally well in advance, and then the team needs to apply it in Identify as they drive the process forward within the judges' target criteria.

An Agreement in Blood

Finish this out with a document that lists the filter and ranks criteria and assigns the name of the stakeholder that created each criteria, along with an explanation for why it exists. Not a committee, not a task force, but a responsible individual. If later on you cannot trace the criteria back to an individual, you are in trouble because you've made it impossible to understand why that criteria was set.

In the venture and private equity world, these kinds of scorecards are the mechanism that drive the investment thesis and keep the partners aligned on the mission. Every corporate executive team has an idea of what is "on strategy" or "off strategy," but it needs to be explicitly articulated, routinely clarified, and documented in an agreement everyone signs.

The agreement is not just from the corporate team but within the corporate team. There must be a cultural expectation that we will be accountable to our agreements and maintain a disciplined approach over time because there are no quick wins. While setting filters, if anyone on your team is saying things like "We just need a quick win," or "We'll know a good idea when we see it," be skeptical. Odds are they don't know what they're talking about.

If, in the process of finalizing this document, you are still left with one or two questions before everyone will sign—great! Partner with the biggest contrarian(s) and get those questions answered or escalate until they're resolved by leadership—quickly. Once this is done and the document is signed, congratulations—you have top-down support. That is the organization's permission to begin, but you'll need bottom-up support to finish.

Inquire Survives from the Bottom Up

We have had a front-row seat implementing NDI in a variety of environments over the last decade. These three multi-thousand-person organizations stand out. All three have had their identities obscured, but those who have lived it with us may recognize an anecdote or two that sounds familiar. All three achieved top-down support from their CEO, CTO, and a few other members of the executive team but then went on to implement NDI in different ways.

In Company A, Merlin received CEO approval to create an ivory tower outside the confines of the organizational P&L. The best and brightest minds from inside the company vied to join the cutting-edge organization as did amazing outside talent. The stakes were as high as the budget—one of the healthiest in the entire industry for this kind of work.

Did I mention they also had approval from the CEO to keep the executive leaders out of the discussion about what they would be working on?

That's the kind of unflinching top-down buy-in this group received since day one. There is wisdom in the closed-door approach—you don't want executive feedback biasing your team to the wrong idea. And the walled garden approach increases the pressure on the secret team to be right.

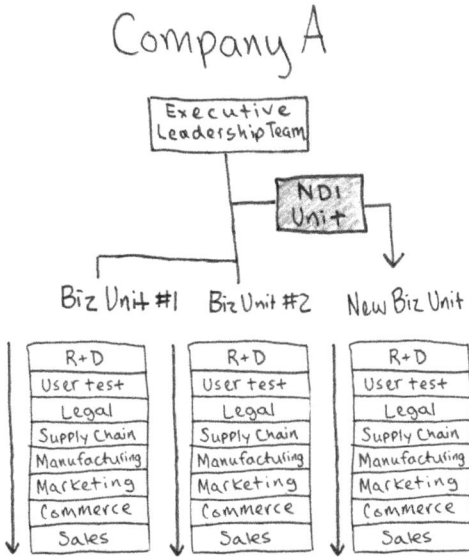

Above all, their biggest challenge is keeping the wolves from other business units away from their budget. When times get tough, why not reallocate funds to revenue-generating business units? Merlin and his team are truly exceptional people, but the rest of the organization doesn't develop products in the same way, so it's hard for them to understand what they're doing.

Their second-biggest risk is a CEO change. Ivory towers are impossible to maintain without long-term support from the CEO. So far, so good though—Merlin and his team are about to launch an entirely new business unit.

In Company B, Guinevere worked for the CTO. She had touch points across a variety of business units that orbit the corporate mothership where she worked. Best of all, Guinevere had her own budget allocated to increasing innovation across the company—which she offered to business units to pay for NDI boot camps. Over the course of five years, she worked with NDI experts and business unit leaders to put on hackathon-style sessions at twelve different company locations. Without creating a specific NDI team, NDI organically became part of company culture; the boot camps gave enough people a common understanding. Countless products were subsequently developed using insights gained with NDI, and a few could even directly trace their origins to a boot camp.

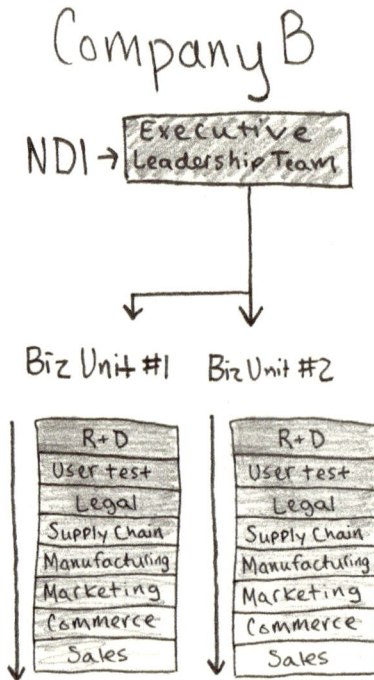

Company B

NDI → Executive Leadership Team

Biz Unit #1

| R+D |
| User test |
| Legal |
| Supply Chain |
| Manufacturing |
| Marketing |
| Commerce |
| Sales |

Biz Unit #2

| R+D |
| User test |
| Legal |
| Supply Chain |
| Manufacturing |
| Marketing |
| Commerce |
| Sales |

One business unit that tracked their product development pre- and post-NDI noted that the number of projects they were working on pre-NDI was more than double the number they were working on post-NDI—that meant fewer WOMBATs. They also noted that the value of their innovation pipeline had almost doubled as they worked on more valuable activities by default. Employee satisfaction and retention improved, as staff shared an almost-tangible belief that they were working on the right strategy.

Just before Guinevere retired, NDI was incorporated into the stage-gate methodology by which all upstream product development was conducted from then on at Company B. As of this book's publication, only five hundred of Company B's tens of thousands of employees have gone through formal NDI training, and they still run multiple NDI events per year to further expand and reinforce the NDI-based company culture. With Guinevere and the old CTO long retired, organic growth of NDI continues to take place entirely from the bottom up.

In Company C, Arthur received support from a few key executive leaders while others remained skeptical. They had seen innovation processes come and go over the years. So Arthur was only given a modest budget and went to work.

First, Arthur worked with NDI experts to educate a small group of executives and train about twenty additional team members on the basics of NDI. The goal was to create a small coalition of support that understood NDI.

Second, Arthur secured nine months of dedicated time from four people with multidisciplinary backgrounds in sales, marketing, and product development to run an NDI project internally with guidance from an NDI consultant. We'd like to briefly pause and say this: even the best NDI teams don't bat 100 percent, so don't expect perfection from your first NDI effort.

In this case, though, the team did well—very well. They found several projects that business leaders perceive as exciting. The effort was renewed for an additional two years, and now there are almost a hundred people in the organization who use and understand NDI. Some are organically leading their own teams with NDI terminology. With a relatively modest budget, Arthur was able to unite the kingdom.

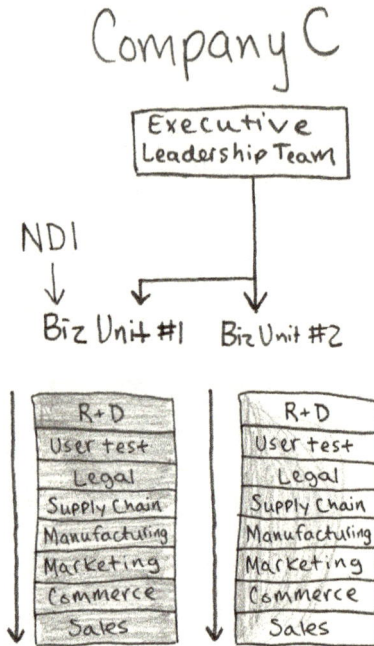

Bottom-up support requires that the organization speaks and understands the same language. Training, boot camps, workshops, hackathons, or whatever you call them are essential to ensure change has staying power. Ivory tower innovation, tiger teams, and the like are effective tools to get results with NDI, but be careful. If an organization isn't ready, the wolves will come, and you'll spend more time defending your strategy than advancing it. Bottom-up buy-in is about establishing a reason for the organization to believe there is a repeatable process to innovate—and for that, they need to see it work for themselves. After that happens, we can't help but smile at what happens next. They want to use it again—they want to innovate—and they never want to go back to the world before.

A needs-driven initiative requires total buy-in, which we've just established. Its survival requires that no one loses faith and kills it. Lastly, the work of NDI happens at the level of the team, which we have yet to assemble. Let's address the team now.

Assembling a Team

Stanford Biodesign's Innovation Fellowship has a deliberate system for their teams. Pulling from MDs, PhDs, and MBAs, they ensure that four functional roles are met. These roles are:

- Builder—usually an engineer
- Domain expert—usually the MD as it is a medically focused program
- Organizer—program management is often run by an MBA or project manager
- Deep diver—a "scientist" profile, usually with a PhD, but commonly found as a competency that exists across most individuals in the program

Because Stanford's program is focused primarily on education and to ensure that each team member receives the same education, the team has no hierarchy. It is a flat structure. Moving a flat structure forward requires constant consensus, which is a feat of conflict management that few teams can pull off smoothly. For this reason, a psychologist is on staff to meet with teams regularly to smooth out that conflict. And as that psychologist can tell you, they aren't always successful in keeping things harmonious.

In the corporate setting, we are concerned with execution over education, and this makes some things much easier. Our NDI team will have a hierarchy, pull from each stakeholder group in the company, and cover the core competencies. The suggested NDI roles are:

- The leader
  - Typically a senior leader or executive in marketing, product, or R&D
- The NDI team
  - Development team member—technical lead
  - Anchor domain expert—determined by area of focus; can be brought in as short-term consultant if not in house
  - Corporate team member—strategy lead
  - Commercial team member—market lead

- Minimum recommended support
  - Program manager—keeps team on task to key deliverables and action items
  - External NDI guide (the sherpa)—guides the team up the mountain. Being external allows honest questions devoid of internal politics, which helps the team get unstuck. Their external expertise can also stoke the team to create fresh ideas.

The leader, like any executive, is responsible for three things:

1. Setting the culture
2. Owning the vision
3. Providing the resources

The leader is not scheduling the interviews, conducting the research, or engaging in the debate surrounding each need statement, so their energy and focus is less likely to falter. When the team is at loggerheads over how to filter, rank, describe, keep, or kill their needs, the leader is responsible for keeping a ten-thousand-foot view of the process and making the difficult decisions that would otherwise stall the team. If the team requires outside support, the leader recognizes what's missing and negotiates for it.

After the leader, an interdisciplinary team is essential. With every key business function represented, there is a person who can translate and advocate for the team's work to each audience. There is a natural touch point for each group on the team. And the members of the team can keep each other on task as the Inquire filters have a natural ownership. This also leverages the expertise of each member of the group and brings resources from their respective departments to bear.

Here's another subtle point on team size: four is the optimal minimum number for the core team. In a two-person group, there is only one relationship possible. If it sours, it's over. In a three-person group, there are three relationships possible, and these groups tend to be a two-versus-one setup, which also causes the effort to sour. In a four-person group, there are six different relationships, which allows for lots of fluidity and makes a stable adversarial setup unlikely. More than four and decision-making becomes increasingly slow and complex. Four-person groups are the best.

Two Additional Rules

Two additional rules for who's on the team—no gaslighters and no assholes. It's hard enough to do NDI without adding damning interpersonal flaws. Everyone on the team must be effective communicators who are trusted and respected by their colleagues. If they're not, they will be ineffective at translating the value of what the team is working on to their outside peers, and whole departments may not trust or value what the team is doing.

Team Member Questions You'll Have to Answer

Attracting people to join this team will vary in difficulty. The incentives for the potential team members must be thought through. Will they be released from their current responsibilities in part or in total? If this project is successful, how long will they be committed to it? If the project moves into development and market launch, will they follow it throughout, or will this be a recurring innovation effort with the mandate to find new markets every quarter? How does this effort fit into the existing system of career advancement in your org? Is this a stepping stone, a cul de sac, or an end in itself within your company? And what is the risk to the current leadership in commercial, development, or corporate that they will not be able to pull these employees back to their department when they need them?

You must answer these questions. If you do not, the uncertainty will build and sabotage the effort. Better to name everyone's concerns, earn their trust, and even enlist them in the solution.

Conducting the Work

The most committed version of this effort looks like this: you have a core team of four people who are full-time on the NDI effort. The team has a shared war room to run the project, they have all read this book (shared language around effort), and they have access to (and agreement on) which digital tools they are going to use.

A less ideal but more realistic version of NDI is that the team is part time, but each member is at least 60 percent allocated to this NDI effort. Part-time allocation to the NDI effort increases the level of difficulty, but this may be the only realistic way to begin the work in your organization. The two biggest problems with part-time teams are:

1. Everyone isn't immediately available at the same time.
2. Each member of the team has a hedge—an outside job opportunity to cling to when NDI gets tough.

Not effectively managing these two challenges can cause the team members to resent each other, and a resentful team will always fail. There is a reason that Sun Tzu, Alexander the Great, Xiang Yu, Tariq bin Ziyad, and Hernán Cortés all united their armies by burning the boats. This is what we are doing; we aren't doing anything else.

For a rough timeline, twelve weeks is the absolute minimum to complete Identify (six weeks) and Invent (six weeks). If something passes those first two gates, you're allowed to advance to Implement. Holidays, vacations, and black swans can and do get in the way, so don't be surprised if a team needs six months to consistently produce results. This can be a big lift for organizations, but it's a necessary one to avoid wasting years and millions of dollars on ideas that should have been pre-identified as WOMBAT.

The big assumption here is that you have already lined up a way to observe the needs of the anchor during the Identify phase. Line up a way to do observations before Identify starts so the team can hit the ground running. If you don't, you incentivize bad behavior, and the team will make too many abstractions before meeting the market.

Reporting Back

We counsel against too much transparency between the team and the executive leadership as the project moves along. Good things can be unpalatable in the beginning, and if we threw them out, there would be few great dishes in the world. So unless you're cooking or cleaning, out of the kitchen. Trust your own judgment that your team will deliver, and sleep soundly knowing you'll have final say before the horse is out of the barn.

But no one likes waiting. It's uncomfortable—more so if reputations and money are on the line. So if you don't solve this conflict up front, here is what happens. The honeymoon period for the new team and new initiative wears off. People are looking for results. Departments that lent their staff are anxious to get them back. People are losing faith and buy-in. Superiors are calling their insiders on the team to get off-the-record reports. Heavy-handed "leadership" starts forcing the team into unwinnable trade-offs. Lines of communication multiply, and agenda setting sidetracks and corrupts the effort. Crash, boom, over. Companies have a two- to three-year memory for these kinds of disasters, and it can take a long time to correct the harm that was done. Like all WOMBATs, let's get ahead of it.

Remind the judges that the focus areas and constraints they set during Inquire are in place to guide the NDI team to identify the best market opportunities without wasting the judges' time. In the beginning, the NDI team will identify a hundred-plus observations that should be whittled down before returning to the judges. This includes applying the judges' filters and rank criteria, calculating an early economic value estimate, and validating the remaining needs with external stakeholders. When there are twenty high-quality need statements, the judges return as collaborators to help the NDI team cut this list down to their favorites but not before. The remaining eight to twelve need statements will undergo deep vetting by the team before a final meeting, where the judges will select the top unmet market opportunities to advance.

During the Invent phase, the NDI team builds a set of market-based criteria that are required for a product to dominate that unmet market. If the unmet markets are again given the green light by the judges, the team will then propose products or services that solve the markets' problems. These will be crudely tested and validated with stakeholders. The next decision from the judges is which of the many available options the company will pursue first and with what resources. As before, the judges will review a distilled list that makes it past their Inquire-based filter criteria and the NDI team's deep diligence of the unmet market's criteria.

The lesson here on communication is simple: tell the judges when and how they're going to be involved before Identify starts.

Don't just report back; make them an integral part of your extended team. But enable the team to make meaningful progress before the judges are brought in.

At the end of this phase, Inquire, it makes sense to review what was accomplished:

1. A full set of internal stakeholder judges has been identified.
2. Their filter and rank criteria for a win are known.
3. A multidisciplinary team has been formed.
4. A way for the team to observe the anchor's problems has been secured.
5. Resources are committed.
6. Timelines are determined.
7. An area of focus is sighted, and everyone is on the same page to begin Identify.

Chapter 4

IDENTIFY: IT'S NO SECRET WHERE THE NEEDS ARE

Everybody wants to be a bodybuilder, but nobody wants to lift no heavy-ass weights.

—Ronnie Coleman, eight-time Mr. Olympia, on market research

Where to Search for Unmet Markets

If you're in the business of solving problems, the most useful feedback is negative. Where is the pain? Frustration? Wasted effort? Where are these complaints loud? For a team looking to innovate, these are fertile grounds, and the first big task is to spot them. If the criteria generated in the Inquire phase answered this question for you, great. But if not—if you have carte blanche to go hunting—where would you start?

You have two options:

- Follow the money (declared markets).
- Uncover the anchor flows (undeclared markets).

In both cases, you'll have opportunities to observe met, partially unmet, and completely unmet needs that could point you toward new opportunities. Ultimately, when prospecting for gold, the easiest place to start is on the land that is already making people rich.

Following the Money to Characterize Declared Markets

We wouldn't be comprehensive if we didn't talk about good old market analysis. It works as a place to begin but an obvious word of caution: declared markets are already known, so using that approach makes it much harder to find new insights. When identifying declared markets, start by understanding the costs at a population level and also at an individual level. For example, we could look up the highest areas of spending in our field of interest. In this case, we'll look at health-care spending on hospitalizations. By the number of people, it looks like childbirth is the biggest opportunity at 3.9 million people. By cost, sepsis is the biggest at $41 billion. Dividing the total cost by the number of hospital stays shows something interesting: per-stay costs are highest for cardiac and orthopedic events—well over double the cost of childbirth. In each of these "markets," you'll probably find lots of valuable needs to solve, some with high-margin solutions.

Top 20 principal diagnoses among hospital inpatient stays, 2018				
Rank	Principal diagnosis	Number of stays	Aggregate cost, $B	Mean cost per stay, $
Top 20 Diagnoses		20,241,886	220.4	12,872
Top Non-Maternal & Non-Infant Diagnosis		12,547,900	179.5	13,711
1	Mother's Pregnancy & Delivery	**3,943,223**	21.1	5,340
2	Neonatal	**3,750,763**	19.9	5,302
3	Septicemia	2,218,800	**41.5**	18,700
4	Heart failure	1,135,900	14.5	12,800
5	Osteoarthritis	1,128,100	18	16,000
6	Pneumonia (except that caused by tuberculosis)	740,700	7.7	10,500
7	Diabetes mellitus with complication	678,600	7.9	11,600
8	Acute myocardial infarction	658,600	14.7	**22,300**
9	Cardiac dysrhythmias	620,000	7.5	12,100
10	COPD and bronchiectasis	569,600	5.3	9,200
11	Acute and unspecified renal failure	565,800	5.4	9,600
12	Cerebral infarction	533,400	7.9	14,900
13	Skin and subcutaneous tissue infections	529,600	4	7,600
14	Depressive disorders	525,000	2.8	5,400
15	Spondylopathies/ Spondyloarthropathy	519,600	12.5	**24,000**
16	Urinary tract infections	508,700	3.8	7,500
17	Respiratory failure; insufficiency; arrest	506,800	9.1	17,900
18	Schizophrenia spectrum and other psychotic disorders	399,900	3.7	9,300
19	Coronary atherosclerosis and other heart disease	358,900	8.7	**24,400**
20	Biliary tract disease	349,900	4.5	13,000

Source: AHRQ, Nationwide Inpatient Sample, 2018

We put "market" in quotes because these haven't met the NDI standard for that word. For example, "sepsis" is too abstracted and too nonspecific to contain any insight. Medically, it means you have systemic immune panic (fevers, racing heart, etc.) as a result of some infectious bug running rampant through the body. But that's like saying someone suffers from "cough"—there are numerous potential causes of a cough, just as there are for sepsis. Many bugs can cause it, many diseases make you vulnerable to it, and all of this varies by age.

Could you imagine a product that would work for everyone in this market? What exactly would you tell an engineer to design for all patients who have sepsis? You can't. It's too broad. Not every person has sepsis in the same way. A deep understanding of this "market" divides it into dozens of subsegments before a homogenous population emerges. It should surprise you not at all that this $41 billion opportunity doesn't contain any real market larger than $5 to $10 billion.

That is why we focus on defining need statements with homogeneous populations that all experience the problem in the same way. So how do you go about finding a market insight? How do you find an unmined vein of gold?

Define Anchor Flows to Spot Undeclared Markets

The marketing world has a concept they call stakeholder journey, which describes how a customer deals with their product offering, moving through the stages of awareness, information gathering, decision-making, purchase, after-sales use, and loyalty. That's not what we are talking about. You need to know the anchor's needs before any of this detail matters.

An anchor flow is the way the anchor stakeholder moves through their problem from beginning to end, considering both mild and severe forms of their unmet needs and all the possible products or services they could interact with along the way. In health care, this is sometimes called the patient journey, and it's begging for an example.

Unluckily, you have a twitchy bladder. Out of nowhere and irrespective of what you eat or drink, you get these powerful non negotiable urges to go to the bathroom. They come throughout the day, and you have seconds (not minutes) to get to a toilet, or you soil yourself. Hell on earth, right? You *definitely* want to work from home. You don't travel. You start memorizing where bathrooms are on your commute and which stores have the best ones. Your life is getting wrapped around this problem, and you think to yourself, *I'm too young for this!* Do some research into the overactive bladder (OAB) market, and you discover the following.

More than forty million Americans meet the criteria, and fourteen million seek initial therapy with behavior changes. Then only four million patients start taking medications. Within a year, 75 percent of patients stop taking their meds. Of the initial four million who take medications, three hundred thousand go on to surgical treatment.

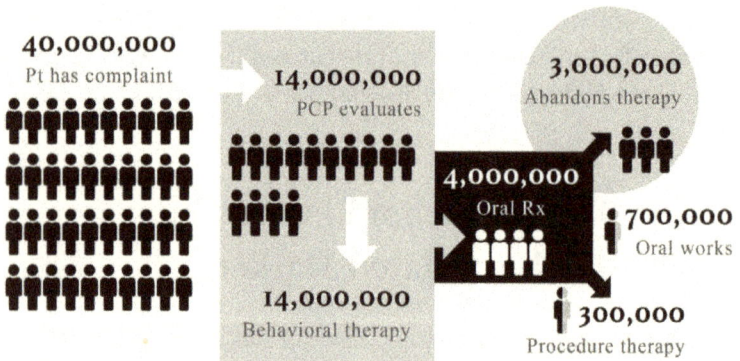

40,000,000
Pt has complaint

14,000,000
PCP evaluates

3,000,000
Abandons therapy

4,000,000
Oral Rx

700,000
Oral works

14,000,000
Behavioral therapy

300,000
Procedure therapy

Why is there a drop from forty million to fourteen million? From fourteen million to four million? Why do 75 percent of patients stop the medications? Are they cured, or could they not tolerate it? Of the three hundred thousand who undergo surgical and procedural treatment, why? Why did others not choose the procedure? What's the story there?

Now notice the costs. The medications range from $80 to $2,800 per year. Why the spread? And the procedures cost between $15,000 to $70,000 per patient. Are people moving between these groups because of cost? Fear? Access?

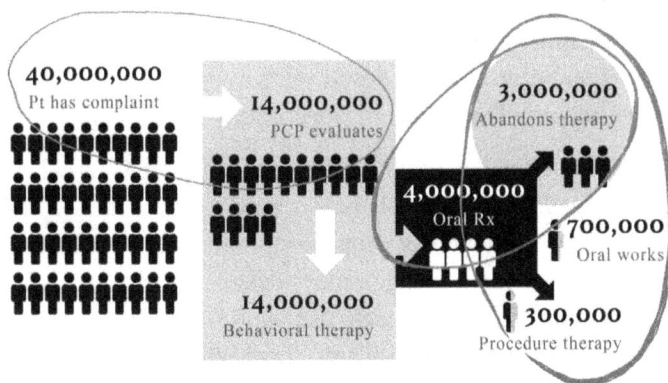

Once you have these anchor flows mapped out and labeled, the areas that deserve focus leap out at you. Unmet needs and unmet markets are hiding here. Of course, it takes more work to find an undeclared market this way, but the reward is less competition and a chance to completely redefine how a category of anchors is served. In our experience, this is the way to more reliable market insights.

Outlining an anchor flow can go poorly if you aren't right about the anchor. This is the main problem we see with the practice of customer discovery. Earlier in the book, we mentioned that we find the term *customer* to be too loose to be useful. Across the four roles of anchor, user, decider, and payer, you might call any one of them the customer. Imagine the market research for OAB if you had instead focused on the surgeon as the customer. When medications fail, some patients move forward with procedures that a surgeon provides. One of these is the implantation of electrodes to stimulate the nerves that interact with your bladder. The surgeon's frustration is that the procedure has two steps: first, you implant "trial" electrodes into the patient and see if they work. If the patient responds, then you go forward with the complete surgery. In your customer discovery interviews, a surgeon might ask, "Can't we make that work for a single procedure?" So off your team goes, working on optimizing a solution for your customer that doesn't move the needle for the 90 percent of anchors who avoid the procedure completely. Customer discovery is useful for iterating on a solution's limitations, but it's not great for identifying the real unmet need that can disrupt the market.

To summarize: unmet markets can be found top down (follow the money) or bottom up (anchor flows), with varying degrees of upfront effort and difficulty. The signals of unmetness to watch for are:

1. Dramatic spike in cost of solving or managing the problem.
2. Change in the number of anchors at one or more steps in the flow.
3. Multiple nondominant solutions are offered, and none seems to work (could be a young or misunderstood market).
4. One established approach that works but that nobody likes because of one or two major drawbacks (like CPAP for sleep apnea or nuclear energy for power generation).
5. Anchors abandoning the current solution and not moving on to try other solutions.
6. Anchors trying to duct-tape their own solution together.
7. Loud complaints.
8. Increase in complications and failure rates. Examples include:
   a. Health care: hospitalizations
   b. Software: high churn rate
   c. Education: poor scores
   d. Military: injury

Seeing with Your Eyes, Understanding with Their Mind

If you want to innovate, it's said that you need to be on the cutting edge or in front or whatever. These analogies are bad. Innovation starts with contacting reality—abstraction is our enemy here. "People say" and "I heard that" and "This report indicates" are verboten from here on out. If you can't say, "I saw it with my own eyes," it's suspect.

So the challenge to your team is to get access to these problems and the people with them. This is why we insist that NDI teams have a subject matter expert, not just because they can translate for the team what the incoming data means, but because they can help provide access to the problems. The doctor can get into the hospital and clinic, the soldier can get into the barracks and outposts, the teacher the school, the astronaut the space station, etc.

Teams stumble here saying, "But they won't let us come and interview and observe!" We've led lots of teams. We know it's hard to get into these protected spaces. Instead of looking at a barrier as a reason to stop, look at it as the thing that will keep your competition behind you once you clear it. We get it done every time. So can you.

Once you have access, your job is to observe and capture. Whether through direct observation (your own eyes and ears) or indirect observation (interviews), what you record has to be verifiable and free of abstraction.

Let's say you're looking at needs in the military and someone records the following: "They need lower-profile ear protection."

The team reviews this and has no idea what to do with it.

"Why did you write that?"

"Well, I saw a team firing a howitzer. They were all wearing electronic ear protection, but one soldier had to hold it in place because it didn't fit well around his helmet."

That's the best version of recovering the observation. Here's what usually happens:

"Why did you write that?"

"That was weeks ago. I don't remember."

Record what happened. "I noticed X; it seemed like Y was important; I wonder if the reason is Z." This is structured as observation (only the facts), perception (your understanding), hypothesis (why you think it's important, testable as true or false). In this way, your team can faithfully review what you've captured, and you have an excellent way of going back to the stakeholder to ask if you got it right or wrong on any one of these different dimensions. This becomes powerful when multiple team members have similar observations with different interpretations.

What would have happened if we spoke with the soldier with the faulty ear protection?

"Sir, I saw that you were holding your earmuffs when the howitzer was firing. It seems like they aren't staying on correctly. Why do you think that is?"

"Oh, I threw my rucksack on the ground and forgot I put them in the bottom. I don't want to get chewed out for requesting a replacement, so I just hold them for now."

Good to know—now we're not going to WOMBAT a solution he doesn't need.

Full-Loop Communication: From Observation to Understanding

Communication is tricky. Most of us fumble our way through it without getting a serious system in place. "Honey, don't forget to buy a dessert for the party" you are told as you walk out the door, your head in the clouds. When you come back home, there is no dessert, someone claims they told you, you claim they didn't, and both are right. This is open-loop communication and is low effort and error prone.

When the stakes are high, this isn't an option, so we see systems emerge. Like *roger*.

If I'm sending you instructions on dropping a bomb, I'd like to know that you received them. Responding "roger" is meant to convey that. It can break down in practice.

"I want no more bombs dropped . . . over." This becomes different with static. "I want . . . more bombs dropped . . . over."

"Roger that" is now scary. The sender thinks they had a faithful communication, and they are wrong. This is an attempt at closed-loop communication, but it falls short. What "roger" communicates is that I received *a* message, not that I received *your* message.

Closed-loop communication takes the form of repetition. The receiver repeats the entire message back to the sender. Once the sender hears their entire message, they say, "Over and out." Sadly, even this fails, which we've learned painfully in medicine.

During a code, when someone is actively dying, it gets hectic, and perfect communication is key. In this case, a patient's heart is beating wildly out of control, and this rhythm needs to be broken. "I want you to give six milligrams of atropine, stat!" the doctor yells to the nurse.

The nurse could just draw it up and give it, but we don't know if she heard the doctor correctly.

The nurse could close the loop, repeat "Giving six milligrams of atropine, stat," and then administer it.

Or the nurse could recognize that this is odd. Atropine is usually given in one-milligram doses. It's usually given when the heart is slow, or there is no beating at all. When the heart is beating quickly, adenosine is commonly given, and adenosine is given at six milligrams. Is this what the doctor meant?

"Doctor, you want me to give six milligrams of atropine because the heart is going too slowly, and you want it to speed up?"

"Oh. No. Sorry, we need six milligrams of *adenosine*. This patient is in tachycardia, and we need to slow it down."

"OK, giving six milligrams of adenosine to slow the heart."

That's what full-loop communication looks like. Receiving *a* message or receiving *your* message isn't good enough; I need to understand your intention. This is incredibly burdensome and obviously is reserved for the highest-stakes communication. You know you're in full loop when you can not only reword the other person and have them agree, but you also understand what they said well enough that you would have done the same thing in their situation.

Millions of dollars. Years of effort. NDI has those kinds of stakes. This is the communication burden we are going to place on you when you meet the stakeholders of your market.

Cunningham's Law is also helpful here: "The fastest way to get the right answer is to share the wrong answer." After your observation, have a discussion with the stakeholder in which you purposely interpret the situation incorrectly. People are piranhas—the wrong answer is blood in the water. It will trigger more activity from them and generate more information for you.

Need Statement Construction

Now that the team has a list of observations that have been validated by the stakeholders, it's time to put these into a form that you can research. For NDI, this is the need statement. It takes the basic form of a need for the anchor population to achieve a valuable outcome (for example, a way to reduce leg movements while sleeping for patients with drug-refractory restless-leg syndrome to reduce the number of sleep interruptions each night).

For most of your observations, you won't be able to construct this, at least not right away. It takes research and insight to understand what the valuable outcome would be. Instead, we recommend starting with an approximate need statement at this early stage with the following modification: a need (desired action on a problem) for the anchor population we observed. The signal that this is unmet is X, Y, or Z (for example, a way to decrease urinary frequency for overactive bladder patients who do not tolerate oral medications). The signal this is unmet is that 75 percent of patients abandon the meds, and only 10 percent of them progress to a procedural solution.

Time and time again, we see teams construct a need statement like this:

1. A way to ultrasound the uterus for third-trimester mothers to determine fetal health.

or

2. A way to determine fetal health for third-trimester mothers with ultrasound.

Let's describe what makes these terrible, shall we? Mothers in the third trimester don't need you to ultrasound their uterus. They need to know if their baby is OK. Putting the modality—the solution—of ultrasound in the need statement completely misses the point. A company that followed this need statement could never discover other ways to check on the baby like fetal pulse oximetry, a physical exam, or any other technology because they are mis-aimed. This means that even if they invented the best ultrasound solution in the world, they could have their entire business disrupted by someone who put the anchor's need first. In the first case, they don't understand what problem they are solving (WOMBAT), and in the second case, they can only consider one way of solving it (also WOMBAT).

You might put a solution into the need at the level of the anchor population. It would look like this: a way to determine fetal health for third-trimester mothers undergoing ultrasound to decrease miscarriage rates.

This sounds a little more insightful because of all the qualifying adjectives in the same way that "small-batch, artisanal, organic summer salad" suggests you shouldn't mind spending forty dollars for rabbit food. The problem with this need statement is that the unmet need is still tied to the ultrasound. If, in your judgment, ultrasound is unlikely to be replaced or changed in the future, well then you can try to innovate within that constraint. But if ultrasound is ever replaced as the solution, no one will have any need for yours.

This has led us to suggest the following rule: avoid putting solutions in the need statement—they narrow the opportunity and open it to disruption.

A second rule to remember: the anchor stakeholder doesn't care about your business.

They care about their needs, not yours. So don't include things your business wants in a need statement. "A way to lower the cost of removing exhaled CO_2 on submarines" doesn't describe an anchor's need—it describes something you want. Something like "a way to remove exhaled CO_2 on a submarine" is their need. Profitability is your performance criteria, not their need.

The work and discussion among the team members to convert your observations into good need statements lays the foundation for everything to come. Your team may end up with two hundred unique observations that they turn into one hundred need statements. That's a great number because it means everyone was working to observe problems in the world. The next trade-off is that the more need statements that move forward, the more work you have to do. One hundred-plus needs? That is just too many to vet. Time to trim the list. To do that, you need to start applying your filters and ranks.

Need Statement Scoping: Trash to Treasure

The most common mistake is to start applying your filters and ranks on need statements that are trash. What makes a trash need statement? Bad scoping: not the same people, not the same problem.

Scoping is making sure that need statements, even when they are in different fields, are aimed at a single homogeneous problem.

"A way to prevent knee pain" is a fake market because knee pain is not one thing with one cause experienced the same way by any group of people. Too broad.

"A way to prevent postoperative knee pain" is getting closer.

"A way to prevent nonpathogenic postoperative knee pain in patients undergoing total knee arthroplasty" nails it.

The economic value (EV) of preventing knee pain might look like a $100 billion market, but that number is a mirage. Not to get too technical, but the knee has many parts—bones, tendons, ligaments, nerves, and so on—and every part can fail in a number of ways. There is no one product that solves every version of that problem for everyone with knee pain. Better to scope down to a true market and get an honest EV of $10 billion. Similarly, the need statement of "a way to reduce birth pain" may have completely missed your observed insight, which should have resulted in something like "a way to reduce postpartum episiotomy pain at home to improve breastfeeding rates at six weeks." Subject-matter experts on your team are essential for this step. Otherwise you might not know, for example, that postpartum episiotomy pain is associated with reduced rates of breastfeeding. Pro tip: do not look up *episiotomy*.

If scoping isn't done before filtering, you will have need statements competing on unequal footing. The unscoped need "a way to prevent allergies" with an EV of $80 billion will beat the well-scoped "a way to safely desensitize anaphylactic peanut allergy in grade school children to avoid emergency anaphylaxis reactions" with an EV of $3 billion, even though one of those is a real market, and the other a vague idea that will fail in later stages. Similarly, the unscoped need "a way to detect cancer for people in order to treat them faster" will filter out because of a lack of technical feasibility, but the well-scoped version of the same need, "a way to provide early skin cancer screening for outdoor construction workers to reduce late stage skin cancer diagnosis," might lead to a huge unmet market.

Need Statement Destruction (100+ > 40)

There is no magic number, so don't create a whole bunch of garbage need statements just to get to 100. Anecdotally, out of more than a hundred teams we have run through NDI, first timers who begin need statement destruction within the 70 to 150 need statement window are the most successful. More than 150 and the amount of garbage is overwhelming. Fewer than 70 and the team doesn't have an aperture wide enough to differentiate a good opportunity from a gigantic one. The small aperture phenomenon is something we commonly see in universities and corporate R&D teams alike. People waste a lot of money, brains, and time working on their first "really good" idea when they could have been working on something amazing.

The goal now is to cut down to forty need statements, and we'd like you to get there with as little work as possible. So let's ask the easy questions first. What is an easy question? Anything in your Inquire filters and ranks that doesn't require hours of research.

Start with your easy filters first. Things like:

1. Does the need support our mission of improving cardiovascular disease? (Yes/No)
2. Is this a patient population we have a sales channel to access today? (Yes/No)
3. Do we understand the mechanism of action that causes the problem (that is, not a science project that will take longer than two years to solve)? (Yes/No)

Remember, filters are yes/no criteria. You should be able to destroy quite a few need statements with a simple set of filter criteria. Best practice? Have a master Excel file with all these needs, followed by a column that labels the reason it was killed. This way, a future team with shifted or expanded criteria can easily pick up where you left off.

Stay away from business model filter criteria like revenue targets for the time being. Those will either be applied after we calculate the economic value or in the Invent phase. Don't work too hard. We're not trying to pick winners—we're just trying to eliminate the obvious losers. Right now our goal is to screen WOMBATs that are easy to spot up front.

Once you have applied the easy filters, it's time to apply the easy ranks. Things like:

1. Commercial risk: How desperate are the stakeholders for a solution?
   a. Green—the market is pulling (desperate need)
   b. Yellow—the market is accepting (people are close to satisfied)
   c. Red—the market is resistant (you're solving a problem they don't believe they have)
2. Development risk: How well is the mechanism of action of the problem understood?
   a. Green—completely understood
   b. Yellow—incompletely understood
   c. Red—not understood at all
3. Market adoption risk: How easy is it to prove you made an impact?
   a. Green—self-evident—no further proof needed
   b. Yellow—testing required but less than one year
   c. Red—more than one year of testing required

With ranks, you need to define your own scoring system that meets your goals. In our example, the assumed goal is to develop a low-risk product the market will quickly adopt. So too many reds will cause anything to be eliminated that the market isn't asking for, is a problem nobody understands, or would take forever to get to market.

That kind of logic is sound but may not always be your goal. The moral of the story is to make ranks that work for you. If your goal is to make new scientific discoveries or to solve problems of underserved and reticent stakeholders, then your scoring system must look different. Your ranks should reflect what an ideal need statement would look like based on the charter you have from leadership for this NDI effort.

If you start with 150 needs, and your filters only get you to 70, ranks are a helpful way to whittle further before calculating economic value. If you apply a few ranks and you still have more than 40—just add another question. Do not ask your team to calculate economic value on more than 40 needs—they will hate you. Fewer than 40 but more than 20 is ideal before advancing.

Economic Value: The Top Forty

Calculating economic value (EV) doesn't have to be complicated. You only require a population number and a cost number. Later on, this calculation will deepen and grow more sophisticated, but we reserve that level of work for things that are worth it. Right now, this shoot-from-the-hip EV calculation is about clearing WOMBATs. Let's start with an example.

Need statement: "A way to keep the bed dry at night for five-year-old boys with nocturia to reduce spend on diapers."

So what's the economic value of solving this need statement?

First, we'll define the cost of what happens when the need is unmet for a single boy:

- Right now, the key economic signal of unmetness is that people pay for pull-ups, and a pull-up costs about fifty cents per night.

Second, we define the number of boys in the anchor population:

- There are around 1.8 million five-year-old boys in the United States.

Third, we define how much of an impact we think our solution will have on the need:

- Girls toilet train three months sooner than boys, so let's assume we can help boys stay dry three months earlier.

So the value of solving this need is:

- [50 cents per night] x [1,800,000 five-year-old boys] x [90 nights saved] = $81 million value

Here is another, slightly more complicated example. The observed problem in this case is that patients in the ICU with central venous access catheters sometimes get blood clots in their bodies at the tip of the device. This stops this critical device from working. So the need is as follows:

Need statement: "A way to prevent occlusions in patients with a central vascular access catheter to reduce the cost associated with maintaining vascular access."

So what's the economic value of solving this need?

First, we'll define the cost of what happens when the need is unmet for a single patient:

- Right now there are two economic signals.
  - A clot-busting drug called Cathflo Activase that can be used when a clot is detected. It costs $240.
  - Alternatively, doctors just replace the central venous catheter with a new one. Doing that costs $366.
  - So the average cost of an occlusion is $306.

Second, we define the number of people in the anchor population:

- There are around five million central catheters in patients in the United States each year.
- About 25 percent of them become occluded during a patient's hospital stay.

Third, we define how much of an impact we think our solution will have on the need:

- We have no idea what our solution will be, but we can make an OK assumption. Cathflo is 88 percent effective, so a reasonable assumption is 88 percent.

So the value of solving this need is:

- [$306] x [5,000,000 people x 25% occlusions] x [88% effective] = $337 million value

Is that it though? Sophisticated readers might be thinking this doesn't make sense because the central venous catheter market is known to be $1.6 billion. The calculation of $337 million is the value of solving the occlusion problem which is separate from the value of the current catheter products. Because you are not doing all the things that a catheter does, you don't get to capture all the value of the catheter market. If you integrate your solution into a catheter—say a clot-busting coating—then the market size will capture the full $1.6 billion and likely grow the market as a result of your product's superior value proposition.

You don't need a PhD in economics to do this. You don't even need to be 100 percent right. You just need to be at least 50 percent right–because you still have forty needs! Your only goal is to eliminate the obvious losers and get to twenty. Record your assumptions and questions throughout this process. You'll need to validate your assumptions and fill in all the details later, but don't waste time on that now. Do that when you have fewer needs.

Some simple mathematical wizardry should show what's worth your time and what isn't:

Need Statement	Economic Value	Thoughts?
A way to improve the speed of blood filtration for patients with end-stage renal disease in order to increase the number of patients having dialysis each day	$9B	Wowza
A way to prevent occlusions in patients with a central vascular access catheter to reduce the cost associated with maintaining vascular access	$337M	Interesting
A way to keep the bed dry at night for four-to-six-year-old boys prone to nocturia to reduce spend on diapers.	$81M	WOMBAT

Another pitfall on calculating value: here, we discounted the value of Cathflo by 12 percent because it is fractionally *effective*. Sometimes, the value is also fractionally *connected*. Let us explain. Your hypothetical company identifies a water contaminant that increases the rate of Alzheimer's disease after twenty years of exposure. You make a product that is 100 percent effective at clearing the contaminant, and the value of preventing Alzheimer's is $100,000 per person. Can you charge $100,000 per person? Not even close. Alzheimer's is multifactorial. Your product might perfectly prevent the contaminant from causing the disease but another factor could ruin the result by independently causing Alzheimer's. Your intervention might get credit for being 10 percent connected to the outcome and top out at a price of $10,000 over the twenty years of prevention necessary. If you insist on a price point that captures 100 percent of the value, you would have to prove that your intervention was connected in a 100 percent manner to the outcome. That means a twenty-year, however-many-person study. It is unlikely that you could afford that study or the expiration of your patents while you await the results. In short, the valuable outcome should have a strong causal link to your intervention that can be measurable in time to matter. This is easiest to demonstrate on shorter time scales and with bigger effects. This is why investors want new products to be ten times better than the competition because this removes the need for long, heavily powered studies to prove value.

These EV pitfalls notwithstanding, it's time to break out those financial filters you defined in Inquire but couldn't use yet. Now that you have an EV, you can start to understand whether the needs would have a reasonable chance of hitting your market size and revenue targets.

Your corporate criteria of "markets with fourth-year revenue projections greater than $200 million" is a great filter, but it's not easy to compare with EV. To do that, you will need to make an assumption of the market penetration rate you would expect by year four so you can calculate the minimum market size required. Let's assume by year four, you'd achieve 33 percent market penetration, which would mean an implied market size filter of >$600 million. That means the EV needs to be bigger—a lot bigger—than $600 million for it to have a chance of meeting your target. Incremental improvements will often have an EV that is smaller than you expect. That means you may have forgotten to include the total value of the incremental solution on top of the existing solution.

For example:

Old need: "A way to prevent occlusions in patients with a central vascular access catheter to reduce the cost associated with maintaining vascular access."

New need: "A way to provide durable central venous access in critically ill patients to enable therapy delivery with long term line patency."

You'll notice that the old need statement had a solution embedded, narrowing it, and the new one doesn't. With this rescoped need, the market changes. Now you can market a product to replace all central line catheters, not just those that occlude. With the old need statement, we could only address the 25 percent of the market that occluded. With the new need statement, you can address 100 percent of the venous access market plus the 25 percent that suffers occlusions.

[$306] x [5,000,000 people x 25% occlusions] x [88% effective] = $337 million value

+

[$336] x [5,000,000 people x 100% of central venous catheters] = $1.68 billion

=

$2 billion upper limit for new central venous catheter free of blood clots

The clot-busting central venous catheter market won't be $2 billion. It will be less than $2 billion but greater than $1.6 billion. At the end of the day, this is about making sure you are in the right order of magnitude. With all the assumptions, nobody should care if the EV is $1 billion or $5 billion, but they should care if the EV is $50 million. It will be obvious what is big and what is not, and that's all that matters right now. We're happy to geek out more on this topic, but that's only for the superfans. So to those who care—reach out. For everyone else, calculating EV will keep you directionally correct by keeping the biggest opportunities in play and discarding the smaller ones. Once you finish, welcome to the top twenty.

Don't Feed the Baby

In the course of the work to come, one team member might make a critical observation or have a key insight that unlocks a promising market—for one need. This need will begin to draw their attention, becoming their "need baby," something they will not let go and will begin to love beyond reason.

This always happens.

If some new discovery or interview draws into question this need baby, the person will argue for discounting it. This behavior frays the team. Even worse, if the need baby survives and becomes successful, the singular ownership of the need will split the team as it is not the team's success. Therefore, as we go through the processes of Identify, Invent, and Implement, we tag each need with the person who identified it, did the market research on it, did the validation interviews on it, etc. And we make sure that the person performing each step is rotated so that:

1. Everyone is familiar in part with every potential market, and
2. Everyone has ownership of every successful outcome.

The Top Twenty

At twenty needs, the level of insight required is not easily researched. This is the time to bring your work back to the stakeholders and get them to help you destroy any remaining WOMBATs. Your work now is to schedule interviews and follow-up visits with the anchors, users, decision-makers, and payers to confirm that what you have so far is directionally correct and accurate. This is where we validate everything.

External Validation

For each of the top twenty needs, prepare a one-pager. It should contain the need statement, your calculation of the economic value (including all assumptions that were made), the anchor flow as you understand it, a list of products/services that are already used, and your judgment of how much the market wants a solution to this need. Your goal is to talk through this document with the external stakeholders and ask them to tell you everything that you got right and wrong.

Do not argue with them, no matter what feedback they give. They may be right, and they may be wrong, but the feedback is their feedback. Check it for accuracy and clarify it later. Schedule at least two interviews per need statement, for a total of forty interviews to be shared by the team. For logistics, you will want two team members present for each interview—one to conduct the interview and one to record. The team member who records often contributes an interesting question to the discussion as the lead team member is usually too focused on maintaining the interview cadence to catch an unexpected answer.

Once the interviews are completed, the team revisits the need statements. Usually, this is a bloodbath, as new information from the stakeholders destroys what was once a promising market. An example from our own experience:

Knee injury and arthritis lead to hundreds of thousands of knee replacements each year. These surgeries have gotten excellent, but most patients continue to put the surgery off for as long as possible. We thought this was because of the high cost of the surgery. It seemed to make sense to us that US citizens were waiting for Medicare to kick in so they could have that insurance pay for it. We thought the unmet need was for a cheaper knee replacement surgery that patients would then choose to undergo earlier.

When we interviewed patients to validate this need, we were told that wasn't their concern. Instead, they were worried about having to go through the surgery twice. Why twice? Because knee replacements historically last fifteen to twenty years before the implant starts to fail. Who wants to have this surgery once at fifty-five and again at seventy-five? It's hard to undergo surgery at seventy-five—that's why they were putting it off.

We now thought the unmet need was for a longer-lasting knee replacement. This profoundly changed the economic value of the solution as well as the evidence required to prove the benefit to insurance companies (payers). They're asking for a thirty-year-long clinical trial? No, thanks. We ultimately killed the need based on this feedback.

Internal Validation

After external validation, it's common for several of your need statements to undergo refinement or retirement. Now it's time to bring in the internal stakeholders, the judges—one group at a time—to help you finish the last set of ranks: theirs.

A word of WOMBAT here—you want pure, relevant, focused feedback on the elements of your need statement research, not the opportunity itself. This means that your market calculations should be vetted by your corporate judges, your competitor research by your commercial judges, your questions about mechanism of action by development judges, etc. Pair the appropriate question with the appropriate audience instead of asking everyone, "What do you think?"

Once you've collected the feedback in part and made appropriate changes with the new insights, it's time to present to everyone as a group and decide what advances and what gets killed.

The goal with the top twenty judges' meetings is to make them part of your process. Their perspective and your hard-earned insights will make for a powerful combination. Share your team's one-pagers with the judges, remind them of their group's Inquire filters, and go to work having them force rank your remaining needs into two buckets—keep and don't.

Some discussion here is good, but don't challenge them too much. Their feedback is the feedback, and remember, you're all on the same team. You want trust and transparency. After all, you still have a bunch of need statements to choose from. Their evaluation is invaluable—it will help you destroy some WOMBATs that you may be too in love with to bury. If you feel strongly that they are wrong or that one of the needs they ranked poorly is actually the best, this is an incredible opportunity to uncover why they feel the opposite way. The signals you might be right are either that there is no data-driven logic to their rationale, or the feedback from multiple other judges is inconsistent or aligns with *your* understanding. Alignment of all the judges makes your life easier. If not, decide if the fight is worth it—with twenty great needs, it's just easier to pick the ones that no one is resisting. A good target out of the top twenty judges' meeting is to cut down to only eight needs.

Don't Hide Your Babies

When teams and leaders get excited by an idea, there is a tendency to try to make it perfect before it's shared with the judges. This is a mistake. Feedback on a half-baked idea is likely to be more honest and helpful than feedback on something that looks "done." If something is already perfect, the only way to respond is that you love it or hate it—this is not helpful if your goal is to improve.

As an example, a large petrochemical company needed to decarbonize their biggest refinery because of their customers' demand for carbon-neutral products. The amount of solar or wind energy required to power their refinery would have resulted in a footprint the size of the state of Rhode Island—not a real option where they are located. They already secured what little hydroelectric power was available in their area, and they still had a major deficit. So what did their engineering team propose? Micronuclear—clean, high energy density, economic, and small—like the kind on submarines. All research and analysis pointed to this as the best solution to their need. There's just one problem.

At the final presentation, the refinery manager cut them off: "I will fire you all before I allow a nuclear reactor to be installed in my facility." Better to uncover this constraint before the final presentation. Sometimes the right answers on paper can still be wrong for reasons unknown to the team doing the work. In this case, the team learned too late that the refinery manager grew up near Three Mile Island—the site of the largest nuclear accident in the United States. If the team had known this earlier, they could have taken a variety of different paths—perhaps even saved their project idea by demonstrating that it could be implemented safely at a different refinery first.

The Crazy Eight

At eight needs, the anchor flow that was mapped previously must be fleshed out by cost and other criteria that the stakeholders demand. Take care to note any unique insights your team uncovers. Each team member takes two of the remaining needs, making sure that these needs are not the ones they worked on previously. We don't want more need babies.

Let's use the overactive bladder example: a way to decrease urinary frequency in overactive bladder patients who do not tolerate oral medications. The signal this is unmet is that 75 percent of patients abandon the meds, and only 10 percent of them progress to a procedural solution.

This has now turned into: a way to control urinary urgency in patients with overactive bladder who are intolerant of systemic anticholinergic side effects in order to reduce episodes of incontinence.

You can see that the need statement has changed dramatically. The assumption was that patients wanted to pee less (decrease urinary frequency), but a member of the team asked, "If you went to the bathroom the same amount but you could control it until you got to the bathroom, would that work?" The answer was yes. The patient's real problem was that they would wet themselves because they couldn't control it long enough to get to the bathroom. "But I also don't like feeling that I am not in control. The panic is so bad that I try not to leave the house, and I can't take long trips to the grocers. Forget about vacations!" So the unmet need is to control urgency.

You also see that the way we describe the anchor population has changed. It's not all OAB patients who don't tolerate oral medications; it is specifically those patients who don't tolerate the side effects of anticholinergic medications. (Some patients fail oral therapy because they can't remember to take the pills, and that is a different need requiring a different solution.)

And finally, we've found an outcome that motivates our anchor stakeholder to want to pay for a solution. The cost of being incontinent publicly is considerable, and the fear of being incontinent limits the scope of their life.

With a solid need statement, we can start to build things out. Let's get laser-focused on our potential market.

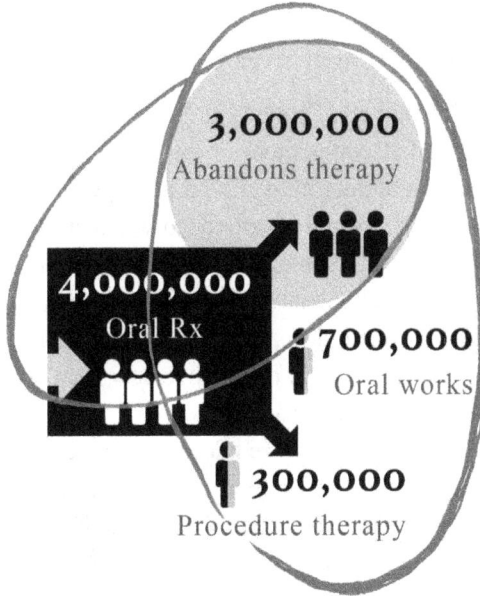

In this example, the critical questions to answer are:

1. What are all the oral medications that these patients are currently taking? Market share, features, and failures must be understood and mapped. What are the characteristics of the patients and doctors who choose these medications?
2. What are all the procedural solutions that these patients choose?
3. Why are people choosing to abandon any of these therapies? What about orals was so terrible, and what about the procedures is prohibitive?
4. How does all this get paid for, and who pays for it?

You want to be in a position where you can account for every person in this anchor flow. These insights are going to inform the entire effort of the Invent phase as you learn the true criteria for what a solution must and must not do. Save yourself time—record this information now. Get religion around validating this with the actual people involved. This is a terrible time to guess when the answer is just a few questions away.

What is the output of this work? You will be able to describe not just an unmet market but a market that is worth getting and can be gotten. Here are the elements you must develop:

1. The need is real and contains an insight–a piece of information that the market competitors do not recognize that allows you to address the unmet market with an edge. You will be able to clearly state the insight in your need statement.

2. The market wants something better. You can clearly explain how all the stakeholders will benefit from a solution. If there is a person who would lose, make sure it is either a competitor or someone downstream in the anchor flow (that is, someone who cannot change the upstream decision).

3. All the stakeholder roles are known. Who are they, and what are their criteria for any solution in order to satisfy the need such that all four stakeholder roles would be aligned? These criteria usually take the form of cost, effectiveness, workflow, and safety/ risk constraints.

4. The market is addressable. You can describe how each stakeholder is identified and can be reached. You can describe whether this is a market that remains distributed (i.e., mass retail) or can be concentrated (center of referral, trade show, etc.). You can describe how money flows with existing products to the person solving the problem. Ignoring existing products, you can describe how money could flow if stakeholders were changed

5. The size of the opportunity is big enough. Assume invention and calculate the economic value available in solving the unmet market. You understand whether this value proposition is cost-saving or revenue- generating to the payer. Are you adding something good or taking away something bad? You can clearly explain how this opportunity aligns with the internal stakeholder criteria defined in the Inquire phase.

Within the anchor flow, there is a market at every node that will either address what is at the node or move the value from one node to another. Not all these markets are worth solving based on your criteria, but the act of learning it is important. At the point at which you have this built up around all your existing products and services, your intellectual property becomes a fortress—you can protect yourself from competition in any direction.

Anchor Flows and Environment

With the anchor flow mapped, it's time to define the best environment. An environment is any location where a solution could solve the anchor's need.

The best place to solve the problem—well, it depends on you.

In our example, a company with an established sales channel in mass retail will logically favor solutions a patient can use at home. A company that sells medical equipment to urologists will favor procedural solutions that a doctor can use in their office. There isn't anything wrong with exploiting your strengths so long as you are also aware of your vulnerabilities. If the problem gets solved at a point in the anchor flow upstream of your solution, your downstream value creation no longer exists. So why not solve everything upstream? Because solving every version of the need at the earliest point is usually impossible because the anchor population doesn't have the same need in the same way this far upstream.

The best environment is where you can solve a homogeneous need, synergistic to the abilities of your company, to create a lot of value and happiness. For some need statements, this means selecting one logical environment, but for other need statements, it isn't wise to choose just one. If you end up with a need that could be solved in more than one environment, great. It gives you more ways to win.

For example, the patients with OAB that can't tolerate the existing medications have that problem in a lot of places. .This need could be solved in an outpatient setting, in a hospital setting, or in a home setting.

But the anchor flow highlights the environments where these patients are with their unmet need: at home and at the doctor's office.

For our OAB example, a start-up may be forced into the urology sales channel because this smaller beachhead requires less fundraising and less capital at risk. A large company with an existing retail business but no dedicated urology sales force might choose to stay in retail (saving overhead costs), though they could also dominate in the urologist's office if they chose it and would then have two channels to develop a winning product.

If you already have a criteria from Inquire that constrains your choice of environment, apply it now and save yourself some work. For example, if a criteria from Inquire says you must use your company's existing sales channels, then any environment outside that sales channel could be filtered out right now. Don't worry if you forget to do this. The judges will have no trouble telling you what is in and out of scope at the next judges' meeting.

We Just Killed Our Favorite Project

Confidence to support—or kill—an idea comes from your experience, skill, and conviction that you are doing the right things in the right way. If you are following NDI and are guarding against WOMBAT, know that the work you and your team have put in will lead you to the right answer, even if that answer is to kill the project. The market must be real. The stakeholders must be aligned. The anchor flows must demonstrate a big opportunity that can be seized. If not, kill it. And when that's your recommendation, you must have a data-driven reason, not just cold feet. The period of maximum fear–when an innovative project is most at risk of being killed–is just before it becomes a self-evident success. Why? Because huge opportunities exist when they are surrounded by problems that no one else has solved. In the Identify phase, these unsolved problems are discovered. It isn't until later that we start retiring them. So don't quit out of fear just before you're about to win.

Top Eight Judges' Meeting

Now that you have confirmed the anchor flows and environment and received feedback from external and internal stakeholders, it's piranha time. Gather the judges and have the team present the results. Start off with an overview of the process that the team went through to get to this point. What was the strategic focus and number of needs reviewed, what external and internal stakeholders have weighed in, and what were the ranking criteria by each of the different internal groups. The team should then present the top eight needs as a recommendation, with the economic values and their key insights. The team should be careful to keep things solution agnostic, but don't be surprised if your judges can't help but think ahead to how you would solve the need. That's a great sign when it happens.

Side note: you want people to be clear-headed, and people are less so over time. The further they get from breakfast or lunch, the more difficult your task. So be smart. If you are talking about line extension opportunities in a category similar to the existing business, this is a low cognitive load for the audience. If instead you are presenting eight opportunities across eight different domains, that's brutal. The team leader needs to shine here by matching the energy of the team to the energy of the audience. If it all gets reviewed in a single two-hour meeting (that's fifteen minutes per presentation), great. If it takes a week with each presentation running an hour, fine. Just don't try to present for eight hours in one go because whatever you put at the end is dead.

At the end of the meeting, it's time for an uncomfortable conversation. We have eight baby birds in the nest, and we don't have the budget, time, or brainpower to feed them all. We have to kick some good opportunities out—not forever, but for now. You and your team will have your favorites—and you should make that known—but ultimately, the judges decide. They will decide not only which need statements will live but also which environment(s) should be your focus for the surviving need statements. This lets you fix your stakeholder roles and begin to establish the guardrails for what you will invent.

The Final Four

Once the judges adjourn, your team has its priorities set. We have seen these meetings push too aggressively to select just one need. This is a mistake. The same is true for keeping all eight. The right answer is to cut several great need statements that the team has worked on for months. If the team finds this uncomfortable, a mental reframing is in order. If you have genuinely great opportunities getting cut, the ones that survive must be excellent. That's the goal. We are not trying to keep everything that isn't worthless—we are trying to only keep things that are most worthwhile. The reason to let go of something great is to keep something incredible.

So congratulations! At this point, you have some amazing need statements. They have stood up to an intense interrogation. They are forged in fire.

Another note: references to one hundred, seventy, forty, twenty, eight, and then four need statements are not exact. Some teams have more, and some have less at each stage. NDI teams have finished the Identify phase with twelve needs that were all amazing and, in other cases, just one. It depends on your goals, skills, and a little luck. Make the process work for you—these numbers are guidelines, not rules.

At the end of this phase, Identify, it makes sense to review what was accomplished:

1. Discovered needs from declared and undeclared markets.
2. Articulated more than a hundred needs.
3. Applied filters and ranks from Inquire on your hundred-plus needs with the help of judges.
4. Calculated the economic value of the need statements and ranked them by value.
5. Validated need statements, the environment, and the stakeholders.
6. Judges have piranha-fied your remaining needs, leaving you with several incredible opportunities that everyone supports.

Chapter 5

INVENT: WHAT'S IN THE BOX?

*If I had asked people what they wanted they would have said
faster horses.*

—Henry Ford, telling on himself

We wince whenever we see someone slap that quote on a presentation or bring it up in a meeting. It's used exclusively by people who think they are brilliant and now grant themselves license to imagine what the market needs. As advice, it's terrible. As a plan? Also terrible.

Needs-driven innovation is a system that allows anyone following it to create the perfect product for an unmet market, and it does so without magic, special visions, muses, or faster horses.

How do we do that? Let's start by disagreeing with more experts. "Think outside the box" is the next casualty of NDI. It's dumb. The goal (we guess) is to encourage solutions that are not tethered to what has come before. The problem is that the most useful tool in the creative act is a constraint. What the market needs constrains you. What the market will pay constrains you. The discovery of new constraints that others missed or old constraints that no longer apply allows you to design the perfect product for your market ahead of your competitors.

Constraint is our friend. We don't want to think outside the box. The box is our friend. We want to think inside the box. To do that, we have to build it.

The Box

The elements of the box are:

1. Environment
2. External stakeholder criteria
3. Competitor benchmarks
4. Financial constraints
5. Execution window
6. Laws and regulations

The magic is that only things that fit inside these constraints will solve our market's unmet need and,luckily, you've accumulated much of this. But what the box isn't is a catchall of corporate restrictions that your company places on itself because you want to use your existing manufacturing or commercial capabilities or what have you. The box is only built by the constraints of the market, and the market doesn't care about making life easy for your company. For that reason, it's ideal to build the box before you brainstorm any solutions to the need statement. If you brainstorm before you define the box, you will be tempted to construct it so that it allows your favorite ideas to survive. In this way lies ruin. The box is the market criteria that define what a solution must do—that's it.

If understanding a question is half the answer, understanding your need statement is damn near the whole thing. The box is the rest.

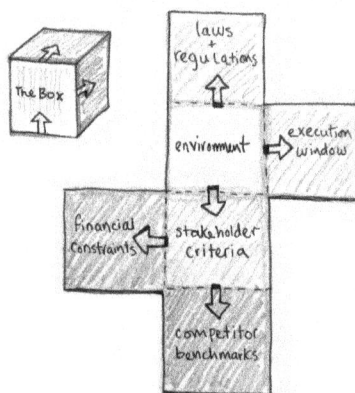

Environment

Where are you going to solve the need statement? Requirements differ when solving in the home, office, field, etc. Everything else about the box waterfalls down from the environment. So when you have one environment, you have one box. When you have two or more environments, you make two or more boxes.

Let's run through a quick example: a way to control urinary urgency in patients with overactive bladder who are intolerant of systemic anticholinergic side effects in order to reduce episodes of incontinence.

The judges said that this was one of the top needs, but they would like you to investigate two different environments in which the company currently plays: mass-market retail and urology offices. A solution that is used at home would dictate a different set of stakeholders than a product delivered in the doctor's office, as this table shows:

	Environment: Home	Environment: Doctor's Office
Anchor	Patient	Patient
User	Patient, caregiver	Doctor
Decision-maker	Patient, doctor (if prescribed)	Doctor
Payer	Patient, insurer (if covered)	Insurer, patient (self-pay)

When stakeholders change, the criteria change. This makes sense. What works in the hands of a trained physician might be too complicated for the home. A delicate instrument might be fine in the office but get destroyed in a purse or pocket. Similarly, the office can sterilize equipment between patients, using one device multiple times. At home, a single-use item might be needed. You can imagine the enormous effect this will have on how each is made and what each would need to cost. This is the effect that the environment has on your solution.

External Stakeholder Criteria

With the environment defined and stakeholders set, you can move forward in defining their criteria. Collectively, the anchor, user, decision-maker, and payer criteria define the voice of the stakeholders in the market. These criteria are what a solution must do to solve the need statement. Any solution that does not meet these criteria will fail.

How do we surface these criteria? We've found the best way to quickly get at this is the piranha method, using existing products. So let's say you're thinking about competing with horses. Find anchor stakeholders who have complaints and start asking them why. They might say things like:

- "Takes too long to get into town."
- "On hot days, the milk spoils before I get back."
- "By the time I bring the ice home, it's water."
- "The closer to the city, the more likely the horse is to spook and rear up on me."
- "It's got a mind of its own. It won't listen to anyone but me. Wife can't use it; kids can't use it."
- "The smell."
- "I don't have enough land to graze it. Have to spend time bringing it to a field every day just so it's healthy when I do need it."
- "Only enough room for me, maybe one other. Can't travel with family like that."
- "I get drenched when it's raining."
- "When it gets lame, either wait months for it to recover or have to put it down."

Are you starting to get a sense of the criteria? Now push back with some other solutions. "What about a horse-drawn carriage? What about owning multiple horses? What about a train? Or a bicycle?" Then listen to their answers:

- "I don't have land for multiple horses."
- "How does a carriage stop the horse from spooking?"

- "What train do you know that comes out to my house only when I want it to?"
- "Bicycle doesn't help me bring anything to market or back."

Now you can take a stab at the filters and ranks you've collected, in order for it to beat a horse.

Dimension/Category	Filter	Rank
Personal locomotion	On demand for time and destination	
Able to carry freight	40 lbs	40 lbs+
Speed of travel	10 mph	10 mph+
Number of passengers	2	2+
Maintenance requirements	1h per day, 2 acres of land	< 1h per day, < 2 acres of land
Number of operators	1	2+
Protection from weather		Don't get wet in the rain
Failure Mode	< 6 weeks of downtime	Duration of downtime
Cost	All-in cost of ownership < 4 horses and a buggy	

If it doesn't satisfy the filters, no one in your market will buy it. After it satisfies those filters, people will evaluate their preference based on the ranks, or how far your solution exceeds their filters. Now go back to the anchor and walk down this list. Confirm every point and take their corrections. This is how you understand the anchor.

Now move on to the user, decision-maker, and payer to create a similar list. The user criteria will specifically guide the engineering team. The decision-maker criteria will guide the commercial/marketing team. The payer criteria will guide the constraints on cost of goods and the business model. At no point will your best idea be "faster horse."

We have noticed that certain categories routinely follow each stakeholder. Here is how we separate these to make them clearer and to help you catch everything.

Stakeholder	What Do They Care About?
Anchor stakeholder	Efficacy, safety (in medicine: beneficence, non-malfeasance)
User	Usability, workflow, learning curve
Decision-maker	Competitor comparison: price vs. efficacy vs. safety
Payer	Value for cost

For all this, you never need to have a product or service. In fact, it's better if you don't. You can always "assume invention", telling people that you have a magic box that solves their problem. Now, follow up and ask people how they would know if it worked and how they would know if it failed. Works like a charm.

Competitor Benchmarking

The most expensive way to learn about the market is to enter it.

It is frustrating, but sometimes, not every dimension that matters is known. Some can be discovered by testing and prototyping the market (which we talk about in the Implement phase), but others can only be learned after launch. The useful thing is that these lessons are often generalizable to all solutions, so general failures of others can help you specifically. This figure describes the experience of a company we know.

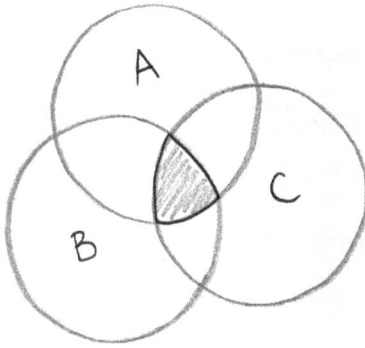

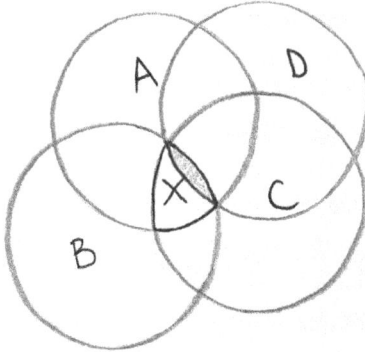

They had an amazing product that satisfied their known criteria (A, B, and C). But as the first entrant into the market, there was a critical variable, D, that was never discovered, and the team learned too late that their product was centered in a dead zone. Luckily for them, they corrected the issue with the next generation. To someone without this company's experience and unaware of D's existence, what they did to change their product might look bizarre or foolish. If so, then that's the kind of fool's gold you want.

Evaluating every competing product and their relative market positions will tell you what the implied criteria are for your stakeholders. Is there a competitor that sells the product outright and another that rents it as a service? Is one feature rich and another feature poor? How well do they work? Assuming that these companies are run by intelligent, motivated people, what is implied about the filters and ranks based on what they are offering? What was their path through development?

Seek out their customers. Find out what competitive products are working for them and why they think they are working. If the feedback from your previous interviews doesn't match what the market is showing you, dive deeper to understand why. Above all else, pay attention to *value*. Your value proposition to your stakeholders must be at least as good as the competition's, or your product is dead on arrival. This is doubly true if you are a smaller company or will be a new entrant into the market. Switching from one product to another is hard. There is friction there. So the smaller you are, the larger your value proposition needs to be to win against a dominant market player.

A common WOMBAT: so far, we have focused on positive criteria–things your competitor does that you must do. There are also negative criteria–things other products do that you want to avoid. When it comes to negative criteria, we've seen teams write endless lists of things the future product cannot do. Cannot cause cancer, cannot cause discomfort, cannot stain their skin, etc. Negative criteria can be a slippery slope—where do you stop? Our simple solution to this is to record only negative criteria that come from reality. So if a competitor product caused a patient to go bald and that hurt adoption, then it goes on to the list. But you will agree that adding "shouldn't cause hair loss" to a new blender is a little silly (though technically true).

A point made earlier but worth repeating: your research into the market must come primarily through your independent observations. Competitive intelligence is valuable but secondary. If you are looking at competitors and iterating on their product, you are also iterating on their assumptions. How do you know they weren't wrong? By the time you see their product on the market, you are already years behind them in development and well behind them in insight. (They know more about their product's failures than you do.)

Financial Constraints

Remember how much fun it was to calculate economic value for your need statement? The last time we did this, it was as a filtering mechanism to get rid of the clear losers. This time, we are going to become more exact because instead of a filter, we now need a target. That target is the commercial value, or what a solution is worth to the market in terms of how much they will pay you for it.

Time for an example. You may remember our dialysis need statement: a way to improve the speed of blood filtration for patients with end-stage renal disease in order to increase the number of patients having dialysis each day.

If you can remember all the way back to Chapter 1, this is the same need statement we said resulted in a failed business even though it had an economic value of $5.6 billion. But in Chapter 4, we said the value of solving this need was $9 billion. How could that be?

In Chapter 1, the assumption was that our fancy system would speed up dialysis by thirty minutes. That resulted in the following value calculation:

[3 dialysis sessions per week x 52 weeks in a year] x [600,000 people on dialysis] x [$2 per minute on dialysis x 30 minutes saved by the magic machine] = $5.6 billion value

The reason this business failed was that the calculation above assumes the dialysis center can do something with the time saved. The dialysis center is the decision-maker, and if they don't make money, they are not going to lift a finger.

An average dialysis session takes about four hours, and with two eight-hour shifts, that means four people at most can sit in the same dialysis chair over the course of a day. Saving thirty minutes for each person would only give the dialysis center a combined two hours of time—not enough time to put another person in the chair. Dialysis centers don't get paid by insurers for doing dialysis on half a person, so the value to them is *zero*.

Now, of course, a solution like this would have value to patients, and maybe some patients would pay a little extra to get some of their time back. But instead of fighting over that miniscule market, why not figure out how much time you would have to save to make it worthwhile to everyone?

Adjusting the performance up to make dialysis forty-eight minutes faster yields the following value:

[3 dialysis sessions per week x 52 weeks in a year] x [600,000 people on dialysis] x [$2 per minute on dialysis x 48 minutes saved by the magic machine] = $9 billion value

Why forty-eight minutes exactly? If the average length of dialysis is four hours, then the new fancy system you invented just shifted the average down to three hours and twelve minutes. A dialysis center only makes more money if they can fit a fifth person into the chair, and at three hours and twelve minutes stacked back to back, it would take sixteen hours to serve five people—exactly enough time. So any solution must be, at minimum, forty-eight minutes faster to create a business opportunity for dialysis centers.

But what about pricing? What's the financial constraint on how much you should charge? Well, the cost of a dialysis session varies, but let's say $400 per person, and the best centers can make a 15 percent profit. If your fancy solution gets one more patient through dialysis per chair, the dialysis center gets an additional $60 profit. So, you can't charge more than $60, or why else would they use your system? Further, your value of $60 in profit to them for that additional fifth person is spread across five patients or $12 per person. If you split this fifty-fifty with them to give incentive for them to switch to your solution, your system can't add more than $6 in cost to each patient. That is the financial constraint on the price you can charge per person.

And now you know why it's so hard to make a business out of faster dialysis systems. Ouch.

But all is not completely lost; we haven't talked about business models yet. Six dollars per patient per session could add up if your faster system was a permanent reusable fixture over a whole year. With more than

600,000 people on dialysis three days a week, a $6 per-patient fee would create a $560 million market opportunity at $936 per patient per year.

And now you know your financial constraints:

- Priced no higher than $6 per patient per session or $936 per patient per year
  - Your cost of goods must be a lot lower to yield an acceptable margin for your business
- Saves at least forty-eight minutes per patient.

Execution Window

Every market has a rhythm for how products are launched, adopted, and depreciated before the cycle repeats. We know this; you know this; everybody knows this. Mistiming the window can be catastrophic—even if you have a great solution to an unmet need. Chances are that if a need has become apparent to you, there's a risk it's now apparent to any competitors who are paying attention. The execution window is a constraint to filter out ideas that won't land in time.

During the early months of the COVID-19 pandemic, a friend called me (Rush) with excitement in her voice. It was July 2020, four months after travel bans had started. Masks, along with other personal protective equipment, were becoming scarce, and almost all of them were being made in China, where exports were being tightly controlled. Her proposal was to set up a small manufacturing operation for N95 face masks in the United States. She had a colleague in China who could ship two machines over to start making masks by the end of December 2020.

My advice was simple and contrarian—don't bother.

About a week before I received the call, early vaccine trial data from Moderna and BioNTech had started to impress. To me, it seemed like vaccines would become available early in 2021 (they did), and the need for face masks would go away or at least significantly diminish shortly thereafter. Unless you already had a manufacturing operation, you were too late. Remember all the universities, start-ups, and random people who rushed to make low-cost ventilators during the pandemic? Same story. WOMBATs chasing a train they had already missed. The only real winners were the largest manufacturers that could rapidly ramp up manufacturing and the companies that made the vaccines. Those companies already had what they needed in place before the pandemic started. Time is a constraint you must not forget.

That was an example of a short window. When you have a longer window, chasing "breakthrough," "innovative," or "science fiction made real" tech can work, as can products with long development timelines (drugs, computer chips, spacecraft, etc.). The execution window varies by market and by need statement. Completely breakthrough sci-fi ideas must promise larger value propositions to justify a longer timeline. Curing cancer or finding a way to make nuclear fusion sustainable continue to be multi-decades-long marches compared to the hilariously short timelines afforded to designing this year's new batch of Halloween costumes.

We love sci-fi, disruptive science, and breakthrough ideas because those feel like the kind of ideas that will make an impact on the world. You're not saving lives or making limitless cheap energy unless you're pushing the limits of science. But technical complexity does not equal breakthrough innovation. Something is called a breakthrough because of what it accomplishes, not because of how it works. A simple idea that creates huge value will always beat a complex one with an equal or weaker value proposition. You just have to discover the boundary conditions that define what any solution has to do to win.

A word to the wise: don't trash a great need today just because it seems technically impossible in the eyes of your team; they may not have any idea what is feasible and what is not. Our experience has been that almost everything is feasible with enough money, brains, and time. Let's say you run NDI, identify a number of unmet markets, and consider several ways to solve them. The best way might be technically impossible now. Work on that need statement should be paused, the assumption being that the time it would take you to chase all that down would be outside your execution window. But you can revisit it—maybe once a year—and review with engineering to someday find out that the door is open. Just make sure the stakeholder criteria goalposts have not moved before jumping back in. While everyone else is looking for a way to "push" that technology onto a matching need, your company will be in the position to "pull" that technology to a need that has been waiting patiently for it.

A winning solution must work in the right environment, satisfy the requirements of all stakeholders in that environment, beat the standards set by competition, work within financial constraints, and get to the market in time to win.

Laws and Regulations

Depending on your field, regulators may have requirements that will be completely separate from the other stakeholder demands. This is why you will usually see an unmet market in the US or another country that is completely met elsewhere in the world. In health care, you may enter an area of disease for which the FDA has already established guidance testing. For electronics, the NIST and FCC will have guidance on electronics and any object that emits electromagnetic radiation. For all industries that depend heavily on intellectual property protections, the laws around patents, trade secrets, trademarks, and copyrights describe what you can and can't do without rights to that intellectual property. Lastly, governments have additional laws and regulations for every industry that you must follow. What about cloning humans to solve the organ transplant shortage? Last we checked, that's illegal! So that idea doesn't fit in the box.

Real solutions support a business. If a product or service works but doesn't generate value, then it isn't a solution. For most industries, protecting that value proposition means having intellectual property as a defensive moat long enough to ensure a return on the initial investment. If your organization has resources to perform a prior art search, now is the time. There are far more patents filed than products made or companies that survived to test them, so looking at living competitors is never enough. The IP search can also turn up companies that launched, tried, and failed in your exact market. Searching on your need statement and its criteria is a gold mine of insight. We are constantly surprised at how little prior IP shows up when you have an insightful need statement.

Looking deeply into the IP held by your current competitors is also valuable. Look up the patent authors, previous employees, assignment database trail, and previous investors to get the unpublished history of how these ventures fared. These insights have given us an edge in development unavailable to teams not willing to look just a little deeper than a third-party search. Were they able to get broad claims or only narrow ones? Narrow claims suggest that the field is old with broad claims unavailable—this is a great sign. Broad claims scorch the earth for anything trying to enter the market with a similar solution. Having a lawyer involved at this stage to support the team is critical and not only for patents—there are lots of ways to create a defensible moat. For a market to grow into existence, it must be shielded from competitive forces long enough to become a going concern.

If these are not areas of established expertise in your organization, you need to acquire it to avoid WOMBAT. Your solution can't break the law, must abide by established standards, and must follow regulations before it is approved for sale—and that's the box.

Sometimes, It's Schrodinger's Box

Going into Invent with two to four unmet needs doesn't mean you will exit Invent with that number. It's common for things to die in the box. We remind you not to be sad about this but instead to be happy. Better to ruthlessly cull now than to let the market do it later.

Visually, Venn diagrams are helpful.

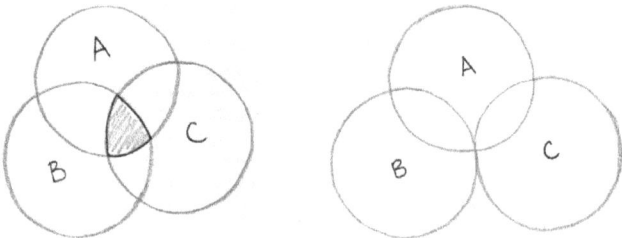

Assuming a simple case in which only three variables—A, B, and C—matter, the winning space is where A, B, and C intersect. If one requirement—say C for cost—is set to something unreasonable, then there will be no space where all three intersect and no solution that satisfies the box. In this example, you have to walk away, no matter how much you are in love with the need statement. This is a WOMBAT.

Another way things fail in the box: instead of building something from the environment, stakeholders, etc., we've seen teams fail by including additional constraints that the market does not demand but that the team wanted to include. Constraints are your friend, but over constraining kills innovation. If your team ends up with all their ideas killed by the box, it is important to go back and make sure that every element of the box came from the market and not someone's imagination.

Time to Discover Many Ways to Win

Invention, it is believed, is creating a solution in your mind that you birth to the world. Nope. Invention is *discovering* the solution. This is why so many inventions feel inevitable in retrospect while no paintings feel inevitable—one is an act of discovery and the other of artistic creation. Like we said in the opening of the book, NDI works for nonartists.

Now that you have the box outlined, it's time to solve within it. Our goal is to have multiple options for meeting the unmet market. At a surface level, it's always nice to have choices. Deeper than that, if you take an idea through development and it fails for one reason or another, the capital-*D* Danger is that you abandon the market. This is what happens with companies that are product first, market second. Once the product fails, there is nothing to fix. In NDI, when the product fails, the market is still there. Still waiting for a solution. Fists full of cash waiting for you to offer something.

When you are certain about the market, if the first product fails that just means the second one is up to bat. So let's build a full roster of hitters.

We break this into concepts that contain embodiments. Concepts are the big bucket, embodiments are related but different ways to solve within that larger concept. Concepts for joining two pieces of wood together might be:

1. Adhesive
2. External mechanical fixation
3. Internal mechanical fixation

Note that each concept is separate from the others with little obvious overlap. We then look at these concepts and think of embodiments that fit into that concept and satisfy our stakeholder criteria.

Concept	Embodiment
Adhesive	glue, tape, epoxy
External fixation	nails, screws, brackets, vise, zip tie
Internal fixation	Dado, mortise and tenon, dovetail

Mentally, you probably have been doing this ever since reviewing the existing products and patent history. People have tried to solve your problems mechanically, chemically, electrically, behaviorally, passively, actively, thermally, sonically, etc. Hopefully, your team has members who can think in terms of these buckets and help sort out what exists already. There are dimensions of force, dimensions of energy, dimensions of human behavior, etc.

Even if none of the concepts and embodiments listed were developed by your team, looking at what already exists and knowing the market's criteria by stakeholder, you should be able to list why each existing product is failing the market and what changes could be made to improve it.

Your team can now create criteria-focused questions for each concept:

Adhesive: How might we (HMW) form a bond that has screw-like strength within sixty seconds?

External fixation: HMW deliver a screw that doesn't rust or cause rot in outdoor use?

Internal fixation: HMW bring the benefits of joinery without the high skill requirements?

Thermally: HMW rapidly join wood products with heating?

And so on.

HMW statements are tools to generate embodiments for each possible concept. HMW was first articulated by Min Basuda at Proctor & Gamble in the 1970s, and further popularized by Warren Berger's 2012

Harvard Business Review Article titled "The Secret Phrase Top Innovators Use."[6] Traditional brainstorming sessions with your team and others are fun and exciting but generate a lot of garbage—this is OK as long as you are using the box to filter out the garbage before seriously considering the ideas as potential solutions.

Brainstorming pro tip: communicate the rules for the brainstorm to everyone.

- No more than fifteen minutes of brainstorming without a break. Lots of short brainstorms are better than a long death march. Your brain will thank you, and space between brainstorms enables you to have more ideas and do more research.

- Invite a diverse group to help you brainstorm—the best ideas can be sparked by naive comments from the inexperienced and the uninformed mixing with people who have deep expertise.

- Nothing kills a brainstorm as quickly as judgment. Judgment is what stops someone with a half-formed, potentially brilliant idea from volunteering it to the group. When that happens, everyone suffers. The goal of brainstorming is not to permit only good ideas, it is to capture a breadth of ideas. That said, we know we can't stop you from judging (at least internally). A productive way to handle this is to force a constraint on yourself which we call "better idea". The rule is simple, you cannot say anything unless you can build a better idea on top of what's been suggested. This way the group avoids judging an idea in real time even when the individual can't. Works like a charm.

Idea notebooks that the team members carry around are great ways to capture the random idea that can strike throughout the day, like the kind you have as you're falling asleep. Outside searches, tech landscape analysis, and start-up ecosystem diligence can show you how those at the cutting edge are working. Going to the local hardware store and looking in a completely different area can also guide inspiration.

---

6 - Berger, Warren. "The Secret Phrase Top Innovators Use." *Harvard Business Review*, (2012). Accessed October 2, 2023. https://hbsp.harvard.edu/product/H009ED-PDF-ENG.

In the beginning of the ideation journey, having a level of intellectual freedom to capture any and all ideas—even bad ones—is helpful. Iterating or combining ideas that won't work can lead to questions and discussions that prompt the team to think differently about what's possible. There are many idea generation methods, from TRIZ to design thinking, brainwriting, and many more, but at the end of all the fun, the only ideas that survive must fit in the box.

The goal for each unmet need that has survived is at least three separate concept families with at least three embodiments per concept. You can go bigger if you want, and that's great for establishing a patent fence around what you ultimately pursue. Just remember that you still have work to do, so the more embodiments to consider, the heavier the lift by the team.

The team can now look back and apply additional filters and ranks and check in with the Judges to down select and approve the most promising embodiments. Pay special attention to embodiments that will delight the internal and external stakeholders while offering up a superior financial value proposition.

Business Models

So far you have a great need statement, its box, and some embodiments that have survived. What you don't have yet is a business. You may be tempted to use the business model your organization uses today, and that's logical. But we recommend at least a slight detour to see if innovating around the business model might give you that extra competitive edge.

Innovating around a business model is similar to coming up with concepts. You have a box that yields a set of criteria that bounds what kinds of business models will be viable.

Let's take an example from "how might we rapidly join wood pieces without using metal?" A glue gun embodiment survived the box. Now we will use how-might-we statements to prompt a discussion of what business models could be possible:

Services: HMW we create a network of certified glue gun technicians who can provide maintenance and repair services so customers can keep their glue guns in good working order?

Disposable: HMW we create a line of disposable glue sticks that are affordable so customers can get the job done without having to worry about cleaning up?

Rental: HMW we offer a variety of rental plans to meet the needs of different customers so everyone can afford to rent a high-performance glue gun?

And so on.

Creativity around business models still has to respect the box. For example, if your business model for a medical device involves paying doctors to use it, you have run *quite afoul* of existing laws and regulations. So whatever model you decide to suggest, check it against the box's constraints before suggesting it to leadership.

Sometimes, in more complex ecosystems, the decision to pay may fall to a committee that uses established purchasing guidelines. If that's the case, get a copy. The decision-maker and payer may have internal incentives by which they are judged. These need to be uncovered. Does the decision happen when one individual says yes, or is there a gauntlet of committees to run? Does the payer have a single budget or a budget that separates capital and operational expenses? Which budget has more room and at what time of year? This may be the difference between a service you provide (operational budget line item) and a product you sell outright (capital budget line item).

Once you have selected a business model, (enabling your embodiment to solve the need and make you money) it's time to check in with the Judges. With their approval, it's time to bend metal.

Prototyping: What's the Question?

Finally, right? You finally get to build something. So what are you going to build?

It's a trick! The better question is "What question are you going to answer?"

If you're thinking of adding a new pizza to the menu of your restaurant, you don't make the pizza. Instead, you add it to the menu and see if people order it. If they don't, don't bother with it. If several do, say, "Sorry, we ran out," and then let the chef know you have a winner. The first question isn't "Did we get the recipe right?" It's "Will people try the pizza with goat cheese and baked cod?"

So what are the critical questions for your unmet need and market? Another trick we use is a premortem. A postmortem is an investigation of a patient after death to determine the cause. But why wait? Instead, we conduct a premortem, asking the team the following: "In one year, it turns out that this embodiment failed. Who can tell me why?"

The way this unlocks everyone's concerns is dramatic. Suddenly, everything the team is afraid to say comes out. Capture it all. This works better when you have more seasoned individuals in the room, so consider bringing in the judges for this. Once you have the list of risks that could kill the project, start ranking them in terms of risk, constantly asking, "What can we de-risk now?" This is how you should approach prototyping.

For example, let's say you are trying to solve restless leg syndrome, a disease where every time you try to fall asleep something in your legs builds to a crescendo of pain if you don't move them. As a result, these people don't sleep and that drives them irritable to mad. You have an idea for a device that patients put on their legs at night. This device stimulates the nervous system, tricking the leg into "thinking" it moved (even though it didn't) with tiny electric shocks. You ask your team for a premortem.

First concern: "What if the tiny shocks wake patients up so they abandon the therapy." In this case you have a scientific risk. Is there a threshold of stimulation that will trigger the nerve without triggering a feeling? According to literature, maybe. You enlist volunteers to have electrodes placed on their legs while they sleep, and your team slowly increases the stimulation until a threshold is detected. If the threshold is above our target of 90 percent of the population, we move forward.

Second concern: "The stimulation won't be consistent on the legs of people weighing a hundred pounds and three hundred pounds." The team collects medical imaging data on skin-to-nerve depth across patients. Sure enough, the distance is different. Is the stimulation needed for that difference still below the threshold? The team returns to collect volunteers and test it. Turns out, it *does* matter. The team then asks if there is a place on the leg that is usually the same thickness regardless of overall weight. Yes, the ankle and the shin vary the least. The team focuses on stimulation efforts there.

Third concern: "The device gets rubbed off during sleep with regular movement, we get inconsistent results, and patients abandon the product." The team comes up with a few different prototypes and asks volunteers to wear them overnight, taking pictures of their legs in the evening and again in the morning. One team uses stickers from the store; one team uses an exercise ankle band; one team uses an ankle brace. The stickers didn't move, but when they failed, they came off. The ankle band stayed in place but rotated around the leg. The ankle brace stayed perfectly, but volunteers complained about the bulk and scratching the other leg. The team further refines the product.

In each of these cases, the team never tried to make "the whole thing" to answer any question. Sometimes they are shocking people with little sticker electrodes; sometimes they are playing around with socks and children's stickers. The point is to answer the risk without WOMBAT. Only after all this is discovered does it make sense to build the product in earnest.

This process often uncovers new design criteria for your specific embodiment. Record these as they become apparent. We'll need this during the Implement phase to take our embodiment and develop it into a true solution.

Potential WOMBAT: Design requirements and stakeholder criteria are *different*. Stakeholder criteria apply to the need and don't change regardless of what concept or embodiment you develop. Design requirements and design specifications are specific for each concept and embodiment, but these never become stakeholder criteria. For example, if you decide to satisfy the horse issue with a service that cheaply delivers oats to horse owners, you may learn that the oats have to be fortified with vitamins. That is a design specification for that embodiment. It would be crazy to add it to the box and then believe that solving the horse issue with Henry Ford's Model T requires you to fill the glove box with thiamin and riboflavin. The Implement chapter dives deeper into the downhill flow of criteria to justifications, requirements, and then specifications.

Embodiment Validation

If your prototype looks "done," you run the risk of learning nothing.

The best feedback happens when the user, anchor, and other stakeholders can readily identify that this is *not* a final product. If they know it's a work in progress, you'll get honest feedback that will be helpful.

Schedule at least three interviews per lead embodiment per need, so if you are working on three needs, each with a lead embodiment across three concepts, this is twenty-seven interviews for your team of four people. Then you'll have the data to know what to change or improve and maybe even enough new insights to help you kill a few ideas.

The goal of the interview is not to have the stakeholder help you invent. You don't want that for IP reasons. Instead, you want them to tell you:

1. If your full list of stakeholder criteria is correct, and
2. In what ways your prototype misses or matches those criteria.

This activity is crucial for de-risking the project further. Set that stage with them up front by spending the first part of the interview on the stakeholder criteria before bringing out the embodiments. Expect to repeat this activity throughout product development until all the stakeholder criteria are met.

Invent Checkpoint

The need statement; the articulation of the box, the concepts, the embodiments, and the business model; and the stakeholder feedback on all of it are going to give incredible weight to your next conversation with the internal company stakeholders. You should now have a formidable, data-driven presentation ready that will excite the judges and inspire them to invest as you bring some of these embodiments into the Implement phase.

At the end of this phase, Invent, it makes sense to review what was accomplished:

1. Created boxes for your needs:
   a. Environment
   b. External stakeholder criteria
   c. Financial constraints
   d. Competitor benchmarks
   e. Execution window
   f. Laws and regulations
2. Discovered many ways to win with several embodiments across different concepts
3. Filtered and ranked embodiments against the box
4. Generated and selected a business model that works for the stakeholders
5. Prototyped
6. Tested
7. Validated to the point you're sure you have a winner

Chapter 6

IMPLEMENT: PLAN, BUILD, WIN

"To think, all that time it was your cup that was poisoned."
"They were both poisoned."

—Dread Pirate Roberts, with a lesson on risk versus uncertainty

Exiting the Invent phase, you should have the following: an unmet market worth addressing. Everyone needs to have the same problem, solvable in the same way, framed as a need statement. You should also have a commercial path toward success and a deep understanding of the four stakeholder roles (anchor, decision-maker, user, and payer) and their respective criteria within at least one environment. And you should have a lead embodiment to solve the unmet need of the market that fits in the box. Preferably, you should have more than one.

But here's what you don't have. You don't have the final product.

No idea survives its first contact with reality. There will be improvement, refinement, and a graveyard. You're trying to see if your idea will work. You're going to make rediscoveries that will make you recycle things you did in Invent. You're going to make new and unexpected discoveries altogether that people didn't tell you because, well, the world did not know that. And now it is *you* on the forefront of discovery.

Your first embodiment may not survive all this, and that's OK. Being wrong about the embodiment doesn't matter when you are right about the market. All you do is move on to a different embodiment within that overall concept or move on to another concept altogether.

But how do you take this forward and contact reality in the best, most efficient, least WOMBAT way?

Most organizations have a stage-gate path they follow for development through commercialization. For example, one company may start with an idea, then move to a prototype. After that, they get user feedback to tweak their prototype's design before creating design specifications that guide development and testing. They repeat this until they get the green light. Then they sort out legal and IP concerns before starting pilot manufacturing and finalizing the product. Once that's done, they move on to manufacturing the product en masse, then marketing it. Then comes sales and, finally, that long-awaited revenue. So it's no surprise there are a litany of late-stage market catastrophes everyone "should have known" with "fail fast" memes floating around.

That seems like a pretty straightforward process. It's the typical way it's done.

Well, it's WOMBAT. Why? For the exact same reason we apply filters before ranks. Filters are cheap; ranks are expensive. The whole point of our strategy is to shift all the risk up front and answer it as early as possible. And if it can't be answered until much later, we have to be sure we have a good way of answering it. Always ask, "Where is the biggest risk hiding?" The longer it hides, the worse it is.

This is not how most organizations approach implementation. Let's look at an example of where this failed—and didn't need to.

How a Good Process Can Fail You

As an example, one company we know created a female sexual health product. They nailed the idea, design, and manufacturing in the expected order, but when it came time to market the product, they were blocked.

It turned out that Amazon, Facebook, and other major marketing channels would not allow the advertising of that type of product. They had run into a brick wall. They couldn't tell their prospective customers, the people with unmet needs they could solve, about their product.

idea → prototype → user feedback → tweaks → green light → legal/IP → user testing → finalization → manufacturing → **marketing** → sales → revenue

Think about the process above. Development was the easy part—the danger was hiding elsewhere. Does it make any sense for them to have buttoned down their manufacturing if they couldn't even market the product? Of course not. But having a static process means you'd spend a lot of money, brainpower, and time on addressing minor risks before hitting the stages that could completely kill a product.

Remember the pizza example? A better path for this company would have been to present a 3D rendering of the product, ask people to join a waiting list, and simultaneously de-risk market access and demand. This would have identified issues with marketing and sales without the WOMBAT of everything that came before.

Why Success Makes It Harder

Successful companies use the stage-gate process because it's a great way to consistently handle development. WOMBAT happens when a truly novel product enters a process ordered by sequential corporate functions instead of by risk.

Why is this more of an issue in larger companies? Start-ups, while trying something novel, are as unburdened as they are ignorant of the normal way of things. It's not surprising they tend to do things in a nonstandard fashion. The forcing function for this is almost always their potential investors.

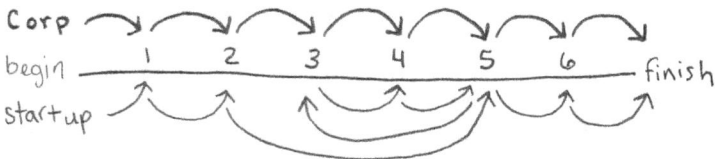

If no one will invest because of a risk at step five, no one cares that you're on step two. They aren't going to fund steps three and four unless you have an answer or early signal on that step five risk. With that kind of pressure, the start-up quickly figures out how to address the downstream risk in a minimal or proxy fashion, or it dies. It doesn't matter if it requires more money or more time or if you have to repeat the steps to get to the finish—what matters is that decreasing the money, brains, and time put at catastrophic risk was worth the delay in achieving the goal.

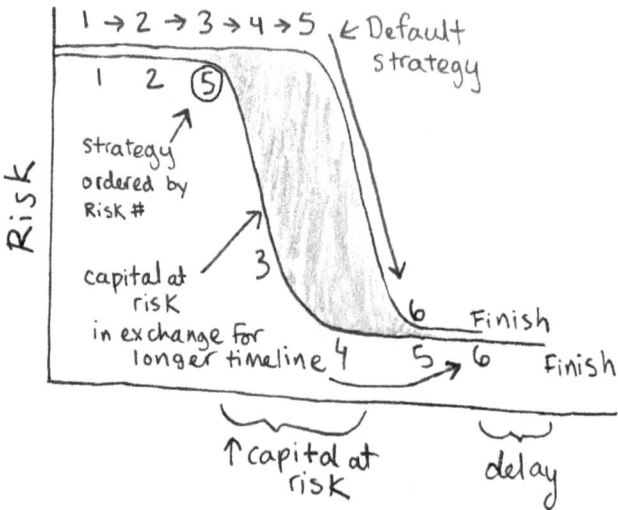

Investors have chosen a career in getting burned, so they are particularly shy of downstream risk. An executive at an established company, by contrast, often enjoys a history of remarkable success. When developing the next generation of products, the focus is on showing that what you're developing is an improvement on what you've already got by ensuring you meet or exceed the established benchmarks. Your biggest competition for funding is other incremental projects and corporate priorities in your company—not your own project's ability to prove it retired its biggest risk. It would be rare for a new risk to surface on a third-generation product, which is the advantage of having successfully addressed an unmet need.

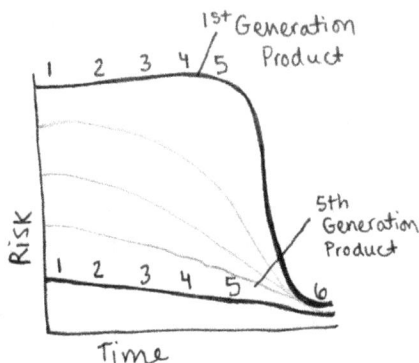

This is why developing novel products causes problems in already-successful companies. But the problem is even bigger than we've let on. A new product, supplier, or manufacturing method represents something more than increased risk. Risk can be handled, but there is something scarier. As Nassim Taleb teaches in *Antifragile*, the scarier thing is uncertainty, and it is very much unlike risk.

Risk is quantifiable and unsurprising. Risk can be priced in. Your quality control process has a 1 percent miss rate, and each error costs $100? You can calculate whether your margins allow you to move forward. But what if your manufacturing process uses a technology that has never been used at scale? You can't imagine what could go wrong. You might think the worst case is the process fails, and you lose a few years tearing it down and establishing more traditional means. But what if the worst case is that it appears fine, but the product, over time, fails catastrophically?

A favorite of ours: in *The Road to Wigan Pier*, George Orwell recounts how the workers in the coal mine prefer the shaft be supported by weaker wooden beams rather than steel girders, which can support far more weight. Why? A wooden prop that is about to collapse gives warning by creaking, whereas the steel fails unexpectedly. No warning means less frequent but worse catastrophes.

That's uncertainty. Surprising and not quantifiable a priori.

This is the difference between iterating on a portfolio product using existing, established methods and building something totally new. Are you talking about risk or uncertainty? Are you de-risking (i.e., getting your quality control system down from a 1/100 miss rate to 1/10000)? Or are you retiring uncertainty (i.e., using traditional materials and methods or extensive tests to failure)?

Typical development makes sense for stages that contain risk only. Projects with uncertainty require a different approach. So we advocate for identifying where uncertainty is likely to hide and reordering development to bring those challenges forward. If this is not done, then downstream blowups are baked into the cake.

After uncertainty graduates to risk, it can be targeted and minimized.

If your project concerns development risks well known to your organization, reordering your normal process is still worth considering. Risk and the costs to minimize it are always determined in terms of money, brains, and time. The unique constraints of your organization determine the best trade-offs to make.

Look at all the questions for an individual embodiment. Try to imagine, with the knowledge you have, which of them carry the biggest risk or uncertainty. Those are the ones you want to test first. After that, you sequentially move down the risk hierarchy you've just constructed until you're ready to link it all together.

The output of the previous phase—Invent—isn't that you have the object you're going to make. The output of Invent is that you have demonstrated that you can think of all the different paths to thrill your market, and you're making an argument for why you think this path has the fewest hazards.

And now? You're going to go straight to the biggest hazard on your path and prove that you can bridge it with what you made. If you can, you move on to the next hazard. If you can't . . . well, that's not the way. But that's OK because your team has the mental ability to think of (and has already come up with) five, six, seven alternatives, all of which still satisfy the box.

The good news is that the majority of risks have already been mitigated by effective filtering. You're avoiding the fate of "We won't know until the end whether or not this worked." For some embodiments, you won't be able to eliminate all risk, but you must understand the size of the risk relative to the reward if you're right. Early MRI machines were like this. You didn't know if they worked until you turned them on, but then you could see inside the body with incredible accuracy. Some risk is unavoidable. So, for opportunities like that, the value must have been damn worth the cost of taking the risk.

Risk downstream does not a WOMBAT make. Risk downstream that ought to have been addressed upstream does. What can now be retired with prototyping? Build for that.

As an example of this, in the early 2000s, GE noticed that patients often felt claustrophobic in MRI machines. So they started investing millions of dollars in a breakthrough technology—a completely open MRI.

Siemens, however, looked at the same complaints. The majority weren't from people with clinical claustrophobia but from people who weighed 250 to 300 pounds. All Siemens did was make their MRI machines bigger.

And Siemens won because they got there faster and monopolized a ten-year replacement cycle, and GE's next generation product couldn't even begin to compete until the Siemens products needed to be replaced. Why? Because they spent too much time building the wrong thing. There was an unmet need for more space, yes, but the solution was not to rethink the machine. Siemens understood this and beat GE.

Overcoming Inertia

A word of warning, however. Often, the process listed above is entrenched in a business's mind. Running down risks out of order in a large organization will cause friction as many of these assets may not be used to being "turned on" out of an established and strict sequence. Downstream marketers may resist being approached before a product is ready for manufacture. This can cause problems.

How can we overcome this?

Well, it's difficult. But we have seen several strategies work:

1. Call in a favor.
2. Escalate to leadership.
3. Leverage gravitas.
4. Throw money at it.
5. Create a flexible process.

Call in a Favor

In a transactional culture, calling in a favor requires that you, as the leader, have "banked" some favors. Long-tenured team players are especially adept at leveraging relationships with colleagues in different departments. Having a fixer on the team with fifteen-plus years of positive relationships at your company can serve you well in soliciting the help you need. Short of this, you may have to wait until the day of a daughter's wedding.

Escalate to Leadership

Escalation to a senior level of leadership is less preferred than calling in a favor because it can burn goodwill. Sometimes, though, it's your only option to get things done quickly. But top-down buy-in can be drained if you over escalate. Don't forget, the leaders you're escalating to will have to drain their bank of goodwill to make things happen, and politics at the executive level, unknown to you and the team, may make escalation as a strategy a bit unpredictable.

Leverage Gravitas

In some lucky organizations, there exists a rare individual with carte blanche to do whatever they want—like a Steve Jobs or a Phil Knight. Steve Jobs was able to grant Scott Forstall (team lead of the first iPad and iPhone) the ability to recruit (steal) any Apple employee from any team at Apple for those skunkworks projects. The reason that Nike was able to land Jordan was that Phil Knight had the ability to unilaterally reallocate the entire basketball marketing budget, meant for four athletes, only to Jordan, an unproven rookie. He also had the ability to approve a last-minute deal-breaking request from Jordan's mother to add a royalty on every shoe sold. Knight had the gravitas to be able to make that happen, forever changing Nike and the entire industry. Nobody else could have made that happen. If your organization has a person like this and they are emotionally invested in your NDI team's success, the world better watch out. You'll be unstoppable, but it's hard to be this unless you founded the company.

Throw Money at It

If none of the above applies, you can always throw money at it. Give your innovation incubator or skunkworks team an oversize budget—but not for them to spend on themselves. The intention is that they use that extra budget to provide support for the actions that need to be done by others. In effect, they become like a grant-making organization to the business, offering money in exchange for specific tasks to be completed. This helps avoid the tyranny of the core business budgeting process at the functional level and enables more flexibility to get innovative things done, especially later in the fiscal year.

Create a Flexible Process

Chances are your organization won't jump straight to changing their company-wide development process right away. That would be a monumental undertaking. Instead, build flexibility into what you have. Classify embodiments as innovative or incremental before Implement begins. The judges are a good group to make this call. If they're incremental, follow the standard process. If they're innovative, then development should be ordered by uncertainty and risk. The judges, with input from the team, will decide the order of uncertainties and risks to tackle. Gate meetings in this process become an interactive forum to evaluate and adjust the task priority throughout development.

In summary, stay thorough *and* become flexible.

The Handoff

Eventually, your NDI team will have to hand off the project to the established functions of the company. When do you do this?

If you hand off your project early, right after the Invent phase, this usually means that the NDI team is dissolved. Now it's production's issue or marketing or whoever. This returns full-time employees (FTEs) to their original roles, freeing up more human capital to work on other projects at the cost of losing the team's institutional knowledge. Don't do this.

If the lead embodiment you put forward doesn't work perfectly, then it's hard for someone who hasn't been working on this project from the beginning to know how to adapt. They don't know the other paths you charted. For this reason, we always insist that at least one member of the NDI team stays for continuity during Implementation.

If you hand off the project late after all the major risks have been retired, you have a significant advantage. In fact, you have the highest chance of success. The drawback is that you have to devote at least four FTEs to the project for six months or more. While increasing your chance of success, you do have to weigh the cost of those four or more FTEs being away from other work.

While it's easy for us to sit here and say you should wait until the project is completely done before transitioning it to another team, that just isn't reality. How and when to transition depends as much on what budget and personnel flexibility you have as the overall structure of your broader company—we'll get to that in a bit. But first, let's talk about how to successfully pass the baton.

The Design Waterfall

From Box to Target Product Profile

How does the output of NDI slot into your existing language and documentation? First, the easy part—what you give marketing.

This far in the process, you have a need statement and subjective and objective data to support that it is an unmet market and has a large economic value. Your work with the judges means it is on target for the company. Your work in Invent led to a deep understanding of all the stakeholders and the competitive environment the product will enter. All along, you have had support and buy-in from top to bottom of your organization. Taken together, the lift to polish the target product profile document should be minimal.

The Waterfall from Box to Design Control

Engineering can be a little harder to please, but at the end of the day, their most important question will be, "When do we get the design specs?"

All large corporations have something like a system development life cycle (SDLC). It is optimized for transparency, efficiency, and documentation during product development. It also tends to focus on user needs or customer needs. We think this has led to a lot of problems as it causes the anchor, user, decision-maker, and payer roles to get confused. NDI fixes this, but it's worth understanding how we got there.

In 1978, the FDA initiated a requirement for good manufacturing practices (GMP) for medical devices. In 1997, design control and quality system regulations were added. Why did the FDA think the way you design something should be regulated? How can you regulate invention, which is the core of design?

The answer is product recalls. Companies making changes to their next-generation products didn't identify (or predict) the second-order complications. And many were not keeping a detailed record of design history. In an effort to stop companies from making mistakes, the FDA forced them to track the design history of every product. That way, companies would know which parts of the design could change and which could not without putting patients in harm's way. The outcome is that the USA enjoys a superior reputation for safety and efficacy of medical products.

Now for the bad part. The language the FDA used to describe this process is the design control waterfall. At the top of the waterfall... user needs. Why? Because the FDA regulates medical products designed for the user. The fine print of their more comprehensive guidance document only once talks about patient needs:

"Each manufacturer shall establish and maintain procedures to ensure that the design requirements relating to a device are appropriate and address the intended use of the device, including the needs of the user and patient" (CFR 820.30(c)).

Even more interesting is that the FDA does not have a formal definition for user needs or patient needs in their design control guidance (21 CFR Part 820) as of the time of this writing. We don't presume to understand the deepest thoughts of the FDA, but if we had to take a guess, they don't have the terms to articulate the difference between the anchor and user requirements, especially with how that changes depending on whether those roles are held by the same or different people.

Because the output of their design and implementation process has to sync with the FDA's requirements and language, almost every Fortune 500 health-care company thinks in terms of user needs; sometimes customer needs; and, rarely, patient needs in their product design documentation. We have worked with a few companies that have jumbled all user, customer, and patient needs together in a kitchen-sink approach. Although thorough, it has been duplicative, incomplete, and confusing.

It's not limited to the FDA. The US Army's quality program, or at least the version from 2018 that isn't classified, doesn't use words like *warfighter*, *soldier*, or even *user*. The word they use to define the person or entity with requirements the army needs to meet in order to solve the requirement is *customer*. What? Last we checked, a soldier on the front line isn't paying for javelins.

The issue is everywhere. The UL (consumer electronics), the FCC (media), the FTC (commerce), and countless other regulatory organizations support similar well-intentioned but distorting terms. It is no wonder that industries across the spectrum confuse these issues.

There are many companies—maybe even yours—that use terms like *voice of customer*, *user needs*, etc. Everyone is grasping for language that makes sense, and now that you know NDI, it's up to you to help point everyone in the right direction. Every stakeholder matters, but the stakeholder who matters first is always the anchor. Nobody else has a need; they have criteria that must be met to satisfy the anchor's need.

Once you have the right language and understanding of NDI, need statements, the box, environment, stakeholders, etc., translating what you know into the design control process language is a piece of cake. See the diagram below.

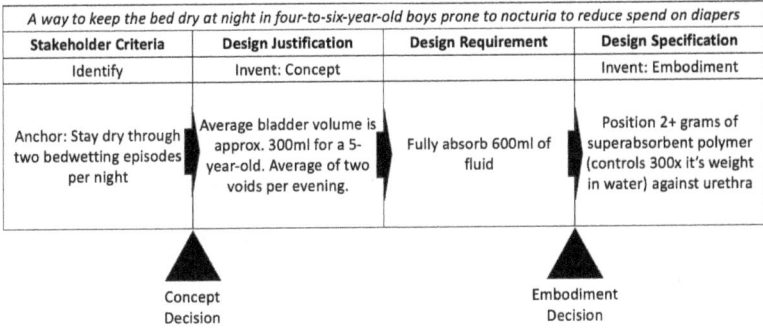

A way to keep the bed dry at night in four-to-six-year-old boys prone to nocturia to reduce spend on diapers			
Stakeholder Criteria	**Design Justification**	**Design Requirement**	**Design Specification**
Identify	Invent: Concept		Invent: Embodiment
Anchor: Stay dry through two bedwetting episodes per night	Average bladder volume is approx. 300ml for a 5-year-old. Average of two voids per evening.	Fully absorb 600ml of fluid	Position 2+ grams of superabsorbent polymer (controls 300x it's weight in water) against urethra

Concept
Decision

Embodiment
Decision

Stakeholder criteria from the box are your ground truth. Once a concept has been chosen, the ways you can meet the stakeholder criteria begin to narrow. You are no longer considering solutions that would decrease the child's urine production, for example. Once you decide to focus on the concept of "control fluid" after it is urinated, you can begin to ask, "How much urine do I need to control and for how long?" This becomes your design justification. In the same way that the Stakeholder Criteria led to your picking a Concept, the Design Justification informs what your embodiment must do (which we call a design requirement) as well as how your engineers will solve it (which we call a design specification). A different embodiment (let's say "child wears a nighttime catheter") would control fluid but would not need to absorb anything because "control fluid" is concept specific, and "absorb fluid" is an embodiment-specific way to control fluid. In the above figure, we've shown what this looks like for a single criteria from the anchor, but this activity gets repeated for all stakeholder criteria and the design specifications that cascade from them.

This may be obvious to you and look just like your company's system. Great! We want this to slot in easily. The key difference will likely be the inputs. NDI pushes you to have stakeholder roles separated so it is easy to see which roles are affected by a design change. If you treat the user and the anchor as one person, an update that improves a user criteria might hurt an anchor criteria. Just imagine a cheaper, more absorbent material for the diaper (helps payer and anchor criteria), but it feels like a rock and is uncomfortable (hurts user criteria and decision-maker criteria). If your company thinks in terms of "customer" (payer/decider) and "user" (user/anchor), your design change will simultaneously help/hurt the customer and help/hurt the user.

Your requirements and design control experts will have their own best way of doing things, but the point here is that your process should start with all four stakeholder's criteria—not just the user or customer.

Business Structures: Functional versus Divisional

How you Implement will deeply depend on the structure of your organization: whether it's functional (segmented off by R&D, marketing, etc.) or divisional (product 1, product 2, etc.). Your business is most likely to lie somewhere between these two extremes, but we'll outline some common pitfalls and opportunities seen with each.

Functional

For functional organizations, the problem of ownership becomes apparent. Who owns the project if each business function is siloed? Who gets the credit? More importantly, who's responsible for it?

The functional siloing becomes its own challenge. Carrying a project across functions is difficult; they're different lands, so to speak. Incentives to work on an experimental project may not exist in certain functional silos. And, given the nature of innovation, working on such an experimental project will be in conflict with the KPIs already established for each functional unit.

Functional Organization

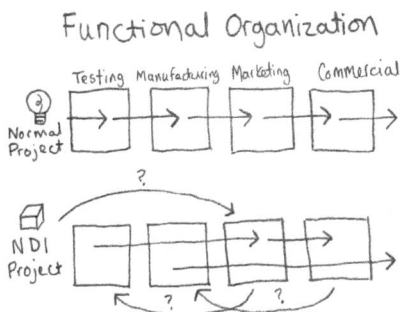

Moreover, what happens when an innovative but high-risk project fails? It isn't uncommon for those people responsible to all lose their jobs. You have to be careful with failure at this point. If the project failed because of negligence or incompetence of the team, then sure—fire away.

But NDI doesn't fail—it kills. If an NDI project is killed, it's for an excellent reason that saves the company money, brains, time, and embarrassment. Lamenting a failure means you think the product should have made it to market—that's fairy thinking. NDI celebrates a kill because the product didn't deserve another second of our precious resources. We don't get rid of people who do something successfully.

The team who runs NDI and stops WOMBATs is saving the company. If leadership rewarded that team with firing them, that would send a clear signal to the rest of the company—a signal that will depress any incentive for people to take a risk. In effect, the nail that sticks up gets hammered down.

However, organizations segmented by function aren't segmented by "turf." Great ideas have the same chance of success because there's little of this turf for anyone to defend. Marketing isn't going to poach from R&D, for example. Nor is production going to try to steal customer service's thunder.

So how do you cross-pollinate? You need a unit outside the organization to own and drive the project across the functions. Marketing can't force a project through R&D. You need someone outside—above—both functions to move projects along. These are the kinds of organizations that generally set up company incubators or advanced technology business units that do not have P&L accountability. It's a big lift, but it can be done in whole or in part. Creating a well-funded ivory tower powered by NDI can achieve success just as much as a more piecemeal approach done over several years.

This requires a human touch, human force. In other words, you need someone (or a team of someones) to leverage their intercompany relationships. It's difficult for mid level and upper managers to do this, but somehow people make it work. It's much easier if you have a C-suite champion in this kind of organization. Easier still if other members or leaders of the functions have been trained in NDI and understand its vocabulary and value.

Divisional

Divisional organizations, on the other hand, are siloed by product or market. This usually means that one or more of these divisions are running their own NDI effort. Sounds great, right? The more NDI going on, the easier it is to find something successful.

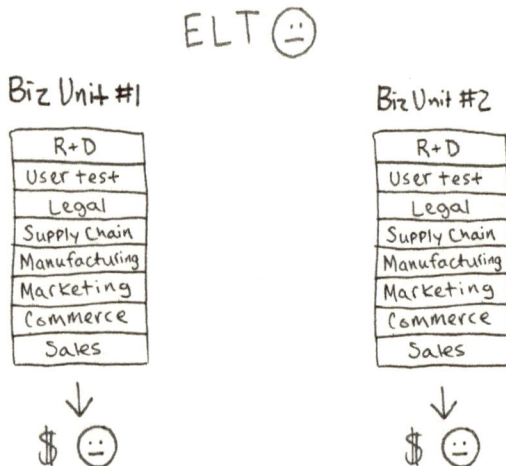

ELT 😐

Biz Unit #1
R+D
User test
Legal
Supply Chain
Manufacturing
Marketing
Commerce
Sales

↓
$ 😐

Biz Unit #2
R+D
User test
Legal
Supply Chain
Manufacturing
Marketing
Commerce
Sales

↓
$ 😐

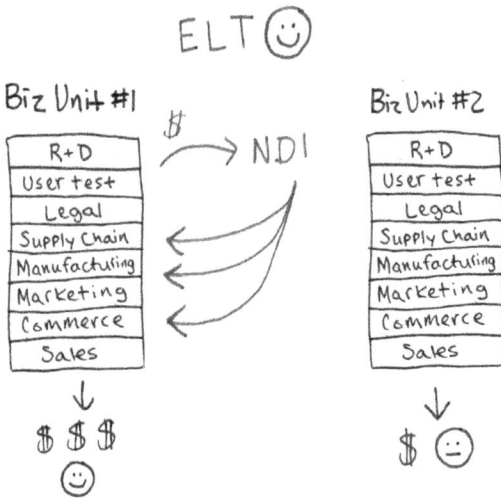

In practice, not remotely. This usually means that a great market discovered by one division is sometimes not shared with another division or is even killed by that other division. Why the hostile behavior? Well, they don't have an incentive to share, so they don't go out of their way to share. But sometimes, it can be killed intentionally to protect one division's budget and resources. After all, one division's success is another's loss. Additionally, the division paying for NDI often sets as a filter at the beginning that the only needs they want to look at are those that fit their business unit. Division narrow, not companywide.

This can also limit the most disruptive options for innovation because, within a division, you are usually tied to just one or a few technology domains. And within a division, you're stuck with one—rarely two—sales channels.

As an example of divisional siloing spelling doom, think of a medical company that attempts an NDI effort. It has three R&D groups; one works on mechanical devices, another works on energy devices, and the third works on biomaterials. None of these R&D groups has ever worked with another before. There's no cross-pollination of research.

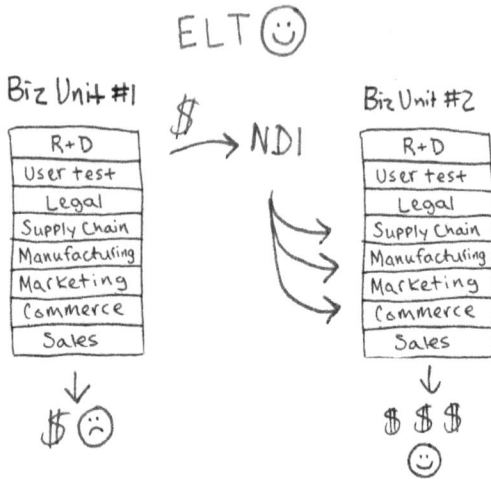

In fact, they are competitive on their budgets and focus solely on solving a need that can be met only with their technology. They're trying to look ahead but fighting each other. Needless to say, that gets nowhere until the structure changes, and they are forced together.

But even with such a limited field, you do have advantages and opportunities. All the internal stakeholders you need exist within a division and are more easily aligned. The issue with the functional silos isn't here. Within a division, marketing and R&D are pulling in the same direction—success in the same market.

Ultimately, NDI may be slow to take off in divisional organizations because there's usually less room for growth or profitability to fund innovation. The division is smaller than the whole of the organization. You might be stuck waiting years before a project is above the line to work on it. So how do you work around it?

One option: have the NDI effort funded above the divisional level, at the corporate level, with filters set to serve the divisions. Like the functional organization, your workaround is to rise above the organizational units. If an unmet market is identified and solvable, then that information should be given to the division to pursue. Then a team is formed within the division, seeded with members from the original NDI team, and the idea taken forward.

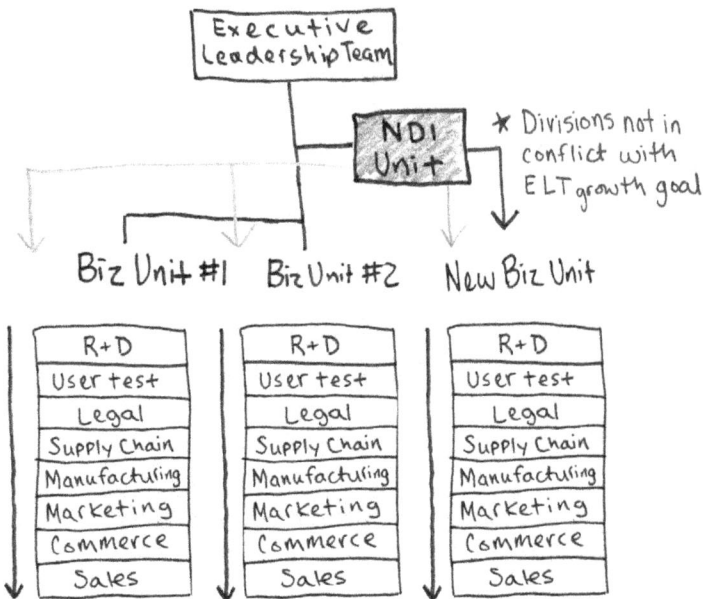

Another option: train the division R&D and marketing staff members to all think in the way of NDI. There is no dedicated NDI team, but in this way, NDI becomes part of the culture. Even for incremental projects, needs-driven thinking can increase product desirability to the market and protect or gain market share. Over time, the division can demonstrate working on fewer WOMBAT projects, which can free up capital to spend on longer-term thinking.

Sure, It's Hard Work. Fobody's Nerfect.

As John Gall teaches in *The Systems Bible*, all systems have flaws. There are no utopias, no codes free of bugs, no statements that can't be misunderstood. Instead, you have to choose which system succeeds in a way you like and has failures in a way you can live with. This is ever true in business. The Divisional structure will excel at getting buy-in but will discard great ideas that don't support the division. The Functional structure allows all great ideas to move forward, but must fight for buy-in to move new-to-world products through departments that would rather build what they already know. The Corporate level NDI team allows all great ideas to survive and doesn't struggle with top down buy-in, but does struggle to get other parts of the business to add work to their already overflowing plates. Like the Dread Pirate Roberts, if you can see these risks early you can survive whichever poison you pick.

Now that we've walked through the NDI process, it's time for a master class in its reverse methodology—what to do when you have an idea first. Like everything with innovation, it's harder than it seems. And it seems pretty damn hard. We'll try to make it easier for you because starting with a technology is a powerful way experts use needs-driven innovation.

At the end of this phase, Implement, it makes sense to review what was accomplished:

1. Defined all the steps required to get to market.
2. Highlighted the steps with uncertainty.
3. Sequentially reduced the number of answerable uncertainties.
4. Sequentially minimized the biggest risks.
   a. De-risked a top embodiment that solves the chosen need statement.

5. Used favors, leadership, gravitas, and money to make things happen.
6. Transitioned the project to the broader execution-focused team in a format that will allow them to catch the baton without missing a step.

Chapter 7

WHEN THE IDEA COMES FIRST

A theory is declared invalid only if an alternative candidate is available to take its place.

—Thomas Kuhn, stating the problem

One must credit a hypothesis with all that must be discovered in order to demolish it.

—Jean Rostand, solving it

I magine there is a pile of treasure locked away in a chest, and you have access to the lock. I'm sure you could fashion a key to open it. You can probe the lock, feel around, shape and hone a piece of metal to match, and voilà, it's open. The reverse is much worse.

Imagine you start with a key. You are convinced that it opens a treasure somewhere. So you just start wandering the Earth looking for the lock that matches it. No amount of failure will convince you that you are wrong about this—you just need to keep trying new locks. Eventually, you're either right or someone forces you to stop.

NDI is treasure first, key second. But sometimes, genius does strike, and the key *almost* fits. This chapter is geared toward that scenario with the goal of helping your idea unlock value.

Due Diligence

When the idea comes first, you are in the same position as any investor. Is this worth the money, brains, and time? Determine if this is an unmet addressable market and if this product is matched to that market.

To research the market, use the proposed idea to form the *implied need statement*. What does this solution do? Who is it for? What value is created?

Just like in the Identify chapter, use the implied need statement to check that the market is attractive and that your company is interested in it. Anchor flows, described in Identify, are a good tool to discover these answers. For ease, here are those checks again:

- Company filters are present. (This may be unclear if you did not go through an Inquire stage.)
- The need is real and contains an insight.
- The market is addressable, and it's begging for a solution.
- The economic value of the opportunity is big enough.
- Capture any stakeholder criteria that have become known.

If the implied need passes the Identify filters, run your solution through the Invent filters. Outline the stakeholders, establish the box, and validate the solution with them.

- Environment
- External stakeholder criteria
- Competitor benchmark
- Financial constraint
- Execution window
- Laws and regulations

For the uninitiated, it is rarer than hen's teeth for an implied need and its solution to survive these two diligence checks unaltered. When alterations to the original idea are required, having a well-characterized, unmet, and addressable market identified is an incredible thing. And having the box well defined guarantees that if a product exists for that market, you will discover it—even if it wasn't your original idea.

But what if your implied need is too small for tailoring? Or your proposed solution will never fit in the box? You're in good company—that's the vast majority of idea-first innovation. In the event that the original idea does not survive Identify or Invent, we've got you covered with these four ways to win.

Types of Opportunity

Type of Opportunity	Solution in Mind	Need Statement Known
White space	no	no
Need first	no	yes
Idea first	yes	Implied from the solution
Platform technology	yes	no

White space is what NDI looks like after the Inquire stage. You have direction and are free to apply the tenants of Identify, Invent, and Implement wherever you see an unmet need.

Need first is what NDI looks like after the Identify stage if you've down-selected to a single need. You proceed with Invent and Implement as described earlier.

Idea first is exactly what it sounds like. Depending on where it came from, it might be attached to an important unmet market. Or not. It might have deep insight baked in. Or not. We've described the work to backfill this information and determine, once you have a full view of the market and stakeholders, if this solution requires tailoring for market-product fit. If the first idea is a WOMBAT that can't be tailored, it's time to reroute back to find a new need statement (Identify) or a new solution (Invent).

Finally, a platform technology already does one job well, and it's your job to find additional markets where it could expand its impact on the world. This is the classic problem of product-market fit. Abstracting the mechanism of what your technology can and cannot do will point you toward multiple new markets.

Rarely a Straight Line

One way we've seen idea first play out is a well-meaning R&D or marketing team member having an idea that skipped the Identify phase. At first pass, it seems like it should work because it's informed by experience and a bit of market or technical understanding. In this example, they had an idea to extend the shelf life of anEpiPen. Keeping the epinephrine as a powder instead of a liquid would extend its shelf life from twenty-four to forty-eight months.

Taking it through the Identify and Invent phases, you discover that your user doesn't have expiring EpiPens in the house. Instead, they tend to buy a few and have them in the car, purse, medicine cabinet, etc. They are more likely to misplace the product before it expires than they are to keep it for more than two years. Add to this that the payer (insurance company) is fine reimbursing on a one-to-two-year cadence, so there is zero economic incentive to extend the shelf life. Longer lasting is a feature—not a benefit.

How is longer lasting, lighter, faster, or more reliable not a benefit? These things are always good, yes? No. Not all features create benefits. A feature is any property of the solution. Benefits are those features that contribute to solving a need. Being lightweight and collapsible may be benefits for a chair, but unless I need a gibbous brisket, the lunar calendar on my meat smoker doesn't cut it. In NDI, these unnecessary features are easy to identify. Any feature that solves the filter or rank criteria of the need creates a benefit. Anything that does not? Worthless feature.

Crucially, maximizing a feature's performance can help solve the need up to a point, after which it may make things worse. Remember the faster horse example? It's good to have a transport that is faster than ten miles per hour. But what qualifies as a benefit up to sixty miles per hour will kill you at six hundred miles per hour. Lighter consumer products feel cheap, and so weights are added. Even making products cheaper can be a liability as purchasers view them as low quality. In each of these cases, a feature of the product is being maximized toward a dead end.

Back to the example. Even though the EverLasting EpiPen should be killed, during the stakeholder interviews the team discovered untrained bystanders (and those in panic) fail to properly give the injection 28 percent of the time when a person is having an anaphylaxis emergency. Eureka! A new signal of unmetness for a yet-to-be-stated need. Since your company is in the EpiPen business, you already know about the market and can write a new, more valuable need statement: a way for any untrained person to rapidly administer epinephrine to a person having an emergency anaphylaxis reaction to prevent death.

Your team validates this need with the external stakeholders and applies the filters and ranks. It not only survives but is also quantifiably better than your original implied need statement. The next stop is brainstorming, when the team comes up with an idea for a talking EpiPen. Like an automatic portable defibrillator, it guides the untrained user giving the injection through the emergency. It's not the original longer shelf life idea, but it saves hundreds of lives each year. Most people will let an old idea go when a better one is in hand.

Platform Technology Innovation

Let's say your company has an incredibly successful technology platform in one market. It's so successful you and another company are the two dominant players. Nothing to do but trade small percentages of market share with each other . . . or is there? Time to find out if there are any other markets to expand your platform's reach.

Let's say you have an innovative tool for treating benign prostatic hyperplasia (BPH), a disease in which the soft gland that wraps around the urethra starts to grow. This makes it difficult to empty the bladder completely, so men end up going to the bathroom more often.

Your system uses high-pressure water and targeted lasers to remove only the problematic soft tissue and leave the surrounding firm tissue intact. The water and unwanted tissue are removed during the procedure. Easy—it's a pressure washer for the urethra. Men with BPH celebrate as they spend more time living and less time in the bathroom.

Your company is slowly dominating the BPH market when the order comes down from the top: "We need more growth, and our initial market is mined out; where next?" Everyone is convinced there must be additional applications for your super cool technology, right?

The first instinct in a situation like this is almost always to expand into different market segments of the same unmet need your technology already solves. But, the reason the technology has been so successful is that it works best for the unmet market with severe disease. Patients with minor to moderate disease have plenty of less invasive and less costly options. So the team recommends developing a lower cost version. This approach is fraught with risk and uncertainty. First, spend money, brains and time to reduce product costs. Second, enter a highly competitive and price sensitive market segment. Then, hope that the customers don't figure out that the cheaper version for moderate disease works just as well as the expensive one for severe disease. If that happens, your expansion market will cannibalize your primary one, leaving you with less revenue and less profit. It's obvious to everyone that it isn't an attractive path but a better one isn't obvious.

Your path to the platform technology promised land starts by understanding what you do well and what you don't. First, define your technology's mechanism of action (MOA) and its constraints in a solution-agnostic way. Why solution agnostic? Because we don't care about your existing product—the only application for it is to pressure wash urethras. We're interested in the underlying platform technology of your product, the pressure-washing cutting system. Our goal is to make a new product that solves a different unmet need while leveraging the same pressure-washing technology. The easiest way to do this is the reverse of what we do in the Invent phase. Instead of starting with a concept and thinking of embodiments to solve it, take your embodiment (product) and abstract it up to a concept.

So we need to define:

- Technology mechanism of action: What does it do, and how exactly does it do it?

- o Concept level: Mechanical separation of tissue based on the tissue's physical properties. Mechanical force delivered by high-pressure fluid.
- Technology constraints: Because of what it does and how it does it, what can it never do?
  - o Must be compatible with water (or other fluid).
  - o Must be OK for cells or tissue in the target area to be spread from the area of use.

Now that you have your MOA and the constraints for your platform technology, it's time to Inquire—with a twist. Find the areas that might apply to the MOA of your technology. Then apply the constraints and Inquire filters to down-select a few areas to move forward to Identify.

Areas That Might Match the MOA	Water Compatible?	Problem if Cells Leave the Area?	Market Pull	Value	Move to Identify?
Orthopedic surgery	2—Yes	2—No	2—Moderate	$$$$	Yes
Adipose tissue/ liposuction	2—Yes	2—No	2—Moderate	$$$	Yes
Tonsillectomy	1—Likely	2—No	1—No	$	No
Brain cancer surgery	2—Yes	0—Yes	—	—	No
Liver cancer surgery	2—Yes	0—Yes	—	—	No
Lung cancer surgery	0—No	—	—	—	No
And more . . .	. . .	. . .	. . .	. . .	No

After prioritizing the top areas it's time to apply what you learned in Identify. It's time for observation, research, and validation of orthopedic and plastic surgeons. Get a surgical understanding of bone surgery and liposuction. Who are the stakeholders in each of those areas; what are the needs, the anchor populations, and the signals of unmetness. Use your technology as a guide for the interviewees to tell you how they would use it. If they say they wouldn't use it, find out why. Is it a deal killer or a clue to what changes you'd need to make to your technology for it to work in this new area? In both cases, you can decide if the market is worth pursuing.

In Identify, your output is a series of need statements with signals of unmetness specific to each of the surviving areas. These needs can be destroyed, valued, filtered, and ranked, together or in their own separate workstreams. When the idea comes first, one of the filters must be that your technology is applicable to the need. You can decide if you want the best need statement in orthopedics and also liposuction or just the overall best need statement. At the end of all the need statement destruction, you will be left with multiple amazing need statements that your platform technology is well suited to solve. If not, you're faced with two possibilities. One, you didn't do Identify correctly, or two, your technology truly doesn't have any other attractive applications beyond its current market. We haven't found either to be common for people who live and breathe NDI.

Now, Invent. With amazing need statements that seem to fit your technology, it might be tempting to stop and jump straight into building a product. Don't. Maintain discipline. To avoid WOMBAT, you still have to go through the steps of Invent. That means building the box and then brainstorming or finding all the concepts and embodiments that may be viable ways to solve the need statement. Don't skip the box. Don't skip trying to come up with an even better embodiment than your original idea.

Pitfalls of Ideas First

We wrote this chapter because, despite our preaching, almost everyone starts with an idea. The goal here is to give companies a way out of the one egg, one basket phenomenon, in which the perception exists that only one idea can deliver a win. With what we've described, there is a way to find a great idea even when starting with a bad one. Below are some examples in which a company could have escaped that fate but fell for a trap.

Wrong Mechanism of Action

A developer of missile defense systems, preparing for the future of warfare, realizes that drone swarms are an increasing threat in the military theater. Already armed with technology that scans an area for airborne threats and launches intercepting projectiles, the developer pivots the platform missile defense technology toward these multiple smaller targets. In many ways, the technological challenge is easier as the top speed of these drones is far lower than that of the missiles currently intercepted. Further, the amount of mass needed for the kinetic kill of the drone is far lower.

The first demonstration of the technology is a success. However, the cost of the projectiles is greater than that of the drones they destroy, so this technology is ultimately rejected after development because an opposing government that could field a drone swarm could wage financial war by depleting capital reserves on the more expensive defensive weapon.

The missile defense developer pushed his platform technology without understanding a cost constraint for the decision-maker and payer. The bidder that won the contract used high-power microwaves to broadly disable a drone swarm, requiring only electricity to function with minimal reload time.

Wrong Environment

If you can remember all the way back to Chapter 1, we talked about a business that made antibacterial-coated medical tubing. About twenty million breathing tubes are used each year during medical procedures and in the ICU, and this comes with a problem. Being on a ventilator longer than twenty-four hours increases your risk of getting pneumonia. And pneumonia kills.

A company has the brilliant idea of coating the tube with an antibacterial agent. They spend tens of millions of dollars developing and testing the product—ending with a seven-hundred-patient study in the *Journal of the American Medical Association*, proving that their tube dramatically reduces the rate of pneumonia. Compared to the regular two-dollar plain tubes, this new coated tube delivers a three-hundred-dollar value for the pneumonia it prevents.

The team had a great technology, a great application, and evidence to prove it worked. It failed because it considered the wrong environment, so the stakeholder analysis was all wrong. This company thought the environment was the ICU because that is where the benefit was realized. What they didn't consider was *when* the tubes were placed. And the *when* determined the *where*.

Many patients are intubated in an emergency, either in an ambulance or the emergency room. Others are intubated in the operating room. Very few are intubated in the ICU. The team made a product for the ICU to place when they should have made it for emergency and OR personnel. If they had done this, they would have discovered that the price needed to be far lower to compete with the two-dollar plain tubes, and this would have meant no possible margin for their device. Further, they would have discovered that no ICU doctor is going to remove a perfectly good two-dollar breathing tube to place a three-hundred-dollar tube since the risk to the patient of losing a safe way to breath is far greater than their risk of pneumonia.

Wrong environment led to wrong stakeholders led to wrong box. That guaranteed the wrong product and a WOMBAT.

Wrong Business Model

Every environment needs a business model that's tailored to fit it. If not, you've solved the stakeholder's problem "technically" but not in a way they can transact with you to solve the need. If their budget incentivizes capital expenditures and punishes operational expenditures, a subscription model will fail when selling the whole thing up front would have worked. I (Rush) learned this lesson painfully when starting Vynca. At first, it was a software-based solution, but 99.2 percent (ish) of health-care IT budgets get vacuumed up by the electronic medical record vendors. An add-on software, no matter how important, doesn't stand a chance. There is no money in the hospital IT budget to pay for it or any of the other hundreds of add-on packages fighting for the scraps. So what did we do? Incorporated a care provider and changed to a services-based business model because reimbursement in health care demands a physical person has an interaction with a patient to generate billing. The software provides enormous value, but inserting a care provider into the model enables the payer stakeholder to activate and pay for the value we provide to hospitals. Different pots of money become accessible through different business models.

Features That Don't Benefit

You've listed the benefits of your product but failed to prioritize them in the way that most appeals to your users and customers. Or you've overlooked some key features altogether. This disorder of benefits allows competitors to disrupt you by presenting solutions and benefits in ways that better match your target audience's priorities (for example, it slices, it dices, it roasts, it fries, but it doesn't fit on a standard kitchen counter).

Solution Agnosticism

Your experience and gut may point you in the right general direction at the beginning of an innovation journey, but you run the risk of closing your mind to innovative possibilities. No matter if you are starting with a white space, a need, an idea, or a platform technology, the magic of NDI is in maintaining the discipline to be as solution agnostic as possible. When starting with an idea or a technology, the goal is to extract the solution-agnostic insights and then quickly reroute yourself back through Identify and then Invent.

By now, we hope you're hooked. This works, it's powerful, and it can save your company. Time to share some of our best kept secrets, hard won from a decade-plus in the trenches of companies using NDI. Look to the next chapter for some advanced NDI tips, tricks, techniques, and tactics that didn't fit seamlessly into any of the other chapters in the book. Some of these you'll be able to use right away.

Chapter 8

CONTACTING REALITY: ADVICE FOR LEADERS

It depends.

—Sun Tzu, being direct

Most of the best advice—the things you should know prior to skipping ahead to this chapter—we've already placed in the appropriate sections of this book. This is, in many ways, the overflow chapter of important things that didn't quite fit anywhere else but are way too important to leave out.

Growing NDI without Killing It

In large organizations, NDI tends to start small. This makes sense—prototype the new process and judge the output before you expand it. When the output of the project is judged by leadership to be worth the time and money invested, awesome! But, the resources may not be ready to scale NDI into its own thing inside the company. Instead it may be kept small for political, budgetary, timing, or whatever reasons—and that's OK, maybe even for the best.

You don't need a team of twenty R&D engineers to jump in from day one. Your NDI teams need to stay nimble and slowly grow when you're confident that the strategy is sound. A bunch of expensive resources waiting around for something to do will cause top-down buy-in to evaporate, and once it does, it takes years before you're allowed to try again. We saw this happen, painfully, at one organization. The CEO was so bought in he wanted everything to immediately shift to NDI. He spent his entire budget (both in capital and goodwill) to pull in all seventy global product development leaders for a three-day onboarding workshop. After that short introduction to NDI, their R&D leadership said, "We can take it from here." In their haste, they skipped Inquire. None of them agreed on what success looked like. The CEO was too busy to get into the weeds, and those at the top of the development organization were too stubborn to admit they needed more help. It wasn't more than a few months before everyone reverted to behaviors that failed them.

The consequences have been catastrophic. The company's market cap dropped almost 40 percent over successive years as a result of still not having a robust innovation pipeline. Worse still, they're even more resistant to anything innovative because after three days... it didn't work for them. Too much too soon without buy-in, and they flamed out.

At the other end of the spectrum is a phenomenon we've witnessed, in which it goes too well and outstrips the resources available at the time. This is especially hard for medium-size businesses to navigate. They're stuck in the middle ground where incremental advances, their bread and butter, leave little time and energy for them to achieve critical mass to do something big.

A successful NDI project gave one such organization growth outside their core domain for the first time in a decade. Everyone became excited and was dreaming about the next big thing. Everything not only becomes possible but also feels inevitable when you have that kind of win. And that's not just in terms of changes in product development but also marketing, sales, manufacturing, operations, etc. Everyone started to believe that their medium-size company can become the next multibillion-dollar conglomerate.

"Can we be more than we have been?"

If the answer to that question is yes, then confidence (and even belligerence) comes with the buy-in to move forward. But what we've seen happen is that all of a sudden, everybody wants to be that disruptive.

Everyone from customer affairs to the R&D team was starving for that bigger dream. A word of caution in that moment: make sure that your finance organization is empowered to say no (or at least guide the staging of investments). IT system upgrade? Marketing rebrand? New factory? Sales team expansion? All become required for the big new innovation vision to succeed. There isn't enough money to fund everything, especially at medium-size companies. Being overly innovative can't be done at the same time as other major overhauls when they all have multiyear payback periods. What about a radical change to compensation and performance structures or taking on debt? This may be a bridge too far. Nobody in an established company wants to miss their bonus, even if you tell them they can get three times the amount the next year. Celebrate your success, but be disciplined enough to hold everyone back unless it's the perfect time to take that big swing.

Risk versus Reward

A successful NDI program tends to keep going. For the business units that donated one of their FTEs for a few months, the work has piled up, and it's time to call the team members back to their regular jobs. In parallel, those team members—even when the project is going well—are pulling themselves in different directions. They're worried about their career trajectory and what that will look like if they don't come back to their "normal" jobs soon. Sure, they're excited and feel attached to the NDI effort, but their heads and their fear say that the waters are much safer where they were, on a repeatable and knowable corporate ladder at a place where they can forecast out for decades where they will be. They want predictability and stability, so they hedge.

The best thing for the NDI effort would be for all the key members to continue until Implement is complete. And, if possible, we advise that this team repeat NDI efforts with new markets. But by the time Invent is complete, NDI team members may feel like the risk versus reward of being part of the effort has reached a sort of equilibrium—especially if this is the first NDI effort in their company. This is the peak time they may try to hedge their way back to their old roles. What a wasted opportunity. FTEs on a successful NDI team should be in prime position to be leaders of the next NDI team or head the new business lines formed when the NDI effort matures past Implement. You need to show them that sticking with the effort skips a few rungs on the corporate ladder to make it worth the career risk of seeing it through. Financial incentives are always nice but rarely the top motivation to wade into shark-infested waters.

If NDI is seen as an experiment in your company, if it's not the way to innovate, then the prospective members may not believe there's a career in NDI at this company when Implement concludes. You can mitigate this by training a larger cohort of executives and role players before kicking off a more focused effort. In this manner, you may even get some unexpected collateral benefits from grassroots actions taken by people not on the NDI core team.

Teamwork Dynamics

You get different results when you hire a commercial leader to run your NDI team, as opposed to an R&D leader. Likewise, product leads will have different outcomes than entrepreneur types.

You can find success with a variety of leaders so long as their mindsets are solution agnostic, economic value is prioritized, and the anchor's need is at the heart of all decision-making.

But what happens when there's strife on your team? What happens when your team keeps exploding, and they don't want to work with each other? What happens when they can't wait to go back to their other FTE because this NDI experience is just a bunch of fighting?

This is the elephant in the room that nobody talked about. Not in the textbook, not anywhere did they talk about what to do when teams just wanted to rip each other apart. It doesn't help that the ground is always shifting under the team's feet.

At the beginning of NDI, the domain expert on the anchor is prized above all other team members. They know all the needs or at least where to look. They have all the insights, and they are what makes the team fly in the beginning. But then, as you get to the filtering, the expert's influence and power start to wane because other topics like economic value, understanding the MOA, technical feasibility, and business models take precedence. At some point, the focus rotates to the commercial and corporate leads.

And even that's short lived. Once into the Invent phase, the developer lead starts to take the reins. And then, with the prototypes developed, it's time to speak with the stakeholders again and—you guessed it—the domain expert comes back to the forefront.

There's all this passing of the baton through the process, along with the interpersonal dynamics and cultural shifts that you have to manage. Baton passing in health care and other industries can create bizarre team dynamics in which disagreeability and agreeability clash. Sometimes, we see engineering teams lose sight of the constraints placed by the commercial and market criteria—especially if they are on a tight timeline or if there is a lack of trust in the quality of the information provided. The experts on the anchor (doctors, teachers, soldiers, etc.) tend to focus heavily on direct experiences that they have or have not had, sometimes at odds with the bigger commercial picture. Meanwhile, commercial team members regularly nudge the scope of what the product can do to be just a little bit bigger, hoping to enter adjacent markets outside the original unmet need. As members of the team tend to steer toward these behaviors, the opportunity for conflict within the team is enormous.

Inevitable Conflicts

In theory, the NDI team you've brought together could and should manage the inevitable disagreements, squabbles, and outright conflict internally. In practice, they need an external locus of control. That locus should be you, the person who's read this book.

In the Stanford Biodesign Innovation Fellowship, each team regularly meets with a psychologist to handle conflict so they can get past personal differences and relational tension to do the work. But you probably don't have a psychologist on staff. And you don't have time to read pop-psych books to figure out conflict management; you need something now.

Here are seven points, principles, and insights that have helped us help our clients (and ourselves) handle team conflict during needs-driven innovation implementation.

Avoid Needless Conflict

We open the book placing stress on a shared language so we agree on what we're talking about when we are talking about it. This problem happens anyway, and so we fall back on the saying that "Words aren't real." What we mean by this is that words are only useful as references to things that are real in the world. So whenever two people have a disagreement and cannot seem to resolve it, make sure that instead of arguing over the words, they at least agree on the things they reference. Full-loop communication solves this.

Is This Conflict Resolvable?

The most damning thing we can say about an opinion or position is that it is "not even wrong". If someone holds a position for which no new evidence would dissuade them, then it is a belief. NDI is an empiric process, not one for unfalsifiable beliefs. A useful rule for us: there will be no arguing until there is agreement on what would cause everyone to abandon a given need statement, product idea, or anything else about to be considered during the needs-driven innovation journey. If nothing would, then it is not even wrong and will be discarded by default.

Missing Variable

When you run an experiment with dependent and independent variables, you assume that you have controlled for what doesn't matter so that you can learn what does. Sometimes, the result is confounding and unexpected. In those moments, you look at the design of your experiment (the materials and methods) for some signal of what went wrong. When all this has been exhausted, you must arrive at the following conclusion: I'm missing a variable in this experiment. Your baby is crying even after you fed her and changed the diaper? The missing variable is sleep. Or colic. Or a hair tourniquet. (Don't look that up.)

So it is with disagreements within the team. You all think you have the same information, but you are not arriving at the same conclusion. What is the missing variable? Ask this, and you will be surprised at the response. It isn't the frame of "Why are you holding on to this stupid belief?" but is instead a frame of "What do you know that we don't?" It quickly unlocks the conversation and results in better team output.

Steel Man versus Straw Man

If you judge someone at their best, you are a sucker. If you judge them at their worst, you're a jerk. Better to realize most things exist in the middle. So it is with ideas. Create a culture in which the highest form of respect is to argue only with the best conceivable point that could have been made. No shooting at a half-baked interpretation of an otherwise fully cooked idea someone else suggested. Bring data, not opinion.

Scales, Not Judges

If you or anyone on your team expresses an opinion on whether something is a good or bad idea, you are passing judgment, which brings the discussion to a halt and suggests that you are not open to changing your position. Instead, if you have to trade in opinion, it's better to adopt the role of an impartial scale that measures and provides objective information. Let's consider an example.

Let's say the topic is knee pain, and someone suggests the transplantation of knees from cadavers into people. Your immediate response is to label this idea as stupid, but that might not be accurate.

There are potential risks involved in such a procedure, such as ensuring a steady supply of cadavers, matching the size of the transplanted knees, preventing disease transmission, and managing immune responses. However, if these issues were adequately addressed, the idea could be a great one. In fact, the use of cadaver tissue in live patients is already well established for ligament replacement in ACL repair and for breast reconstruction.

Now, your team may collectively decide that this undertaking falls outside your risk-versus-reward profile, and that's perfectly acceptable. However, such a decision should be made as a team, after a data-driven discussion, without relying on individual prejudgments.

Celebrate "Failure"

With our clients, we've celebrated when we found dead ends in the process and not in the market. "Thank God! We'd spent all this time thinking we had the right solution, and we finally found out we were wrong. Now we get to work on the correct solution." We celebrate these "timely failures" because we're in search of the even better thing we could be doing with our money, brains, and time. There's no such thing as failure in NDI—failures are when a WOMBAT sneaks through without being recognized. Once this is internalized, the conflicts that come from trying to keep an idea going will disappear, and the focus will be on preventing bad ideas from getting to the market.

Shallows versus Deep Waters

There are two potential reasons for failure in any given team setting, NDI or otherwise—either an individual has not adhered to the team's culture, or the team's culture has not adequately addressed whatever was the issue at hand. In the short term, you'll need an external judge, one who is impartial and does not have any political or other power dynamic—type relationship with anyone on the team, ensuring that the team accepts the judge's decision.

In the long term, you can strive to uncover the underlying paradigms that shape the team's beliefs about how the innovation effort should go. Many of these paradigms are instilled through our upbringing and environment, often unintentionally, making them difficult to notice. A paradigm is a rule for judging the world. For instance, paradigms can be beliefs such as "The world should have order" versus "The world is chaotic," or "People are responsible for their own emotions" versus "People are responsible for how they make others feel." These paradigms, sometimes called invisible scripts, determine how we interpret the world around us—and, in this case, the world around your team as they undertake NDI.

Now, the typical process is as follows: when something happens, we unconsciously check it against our paradigms. If it aligns with our paradigms, there is no conflict or emotional reaction. However, if it conflicts with our paradigms, positive or negative emotions are triggered, and we act based on those emotions. The responses we receive from others then reinforce our paradigms, leading to a spiraling effect.

As a leader, your long-term goal is to bring the unconscious process into the conscious arena, similar to a psychiatrist. Recognizing that individuals are responsible for each step after an event occurs, leaders should empower individuals to change their paradigms. If a paradigm contributes to success, it can be kept, but if it consistently causes conflict, abandon it.

Applying this rather abstract principle requires significant effort from both leaders and individuals. A more practical solution involves establishing a culture based on a set of paradigms that effectively address such issues. This requires careful consideration and planning to create a culture that promotes constructive paradigms and facilitates healthy responses to conflict.

You may not think you have time for this kind of forethought. But you definitely won't have time for it when you need to have already done it.

Explaining Your Team to the Organization

We've already spoken about how the NDI team members will have concerns about joining this new effort. It is a change to their career and carries, with the greater reward, greater risk. What we haven't discussed is how their coworkers will feel. For members of their previous business unit, losing a team member to an NDI effort means picking up the work that is left behind. For those employees who wanted to join the effort and weren't selected, jealousy may arise. You need to have a plan for managing this before it grows.

The way to describe your team to others: they're test pilots.

Test pilots put themselves at incredible risk. If successful, the world leaps forward. Everyone understands that it is a special job and not one that most of us want. Instead, we would like to wait until the bugs are worked out, and we are then happy to strap into something reliable and safe.

The NDI team is taking a risk to see if it works in order to de-risk it for the organization so that, in the future, it is a practice others can repeat. To ensure that this happens, you want the best people in your organization to accept that risk. As for the pilots, the organization needs to make it clear that they will not be judged on the outcome; instead, they're going to be judged on the fact that they got into the rocket and probably flew it as far as it could go.

Success is stopping a bad design from making it to mass production, where it gains the power to destroy the organization.

For these test pilots, hazard pay would be nice, but it's not why they strap in. The secret is that while creative incentives are motivating to some people, the vast majority just want to make a difference. You don't necessarily need an incentive structure that gives somebody a huge payday. If that was all that motivated them, they would be on Wall Street. Instead, what you do need is a structure that lowers the career risk of taking this chance. You need to give credit for this risk on the management ladder while not accidentally encouraging them to jump to another role at a different (or even the same) organization. You need people to stay long term. You need to keep your test pilots healthy and flying so they can eventually lead the next generation.

Let Your Test Pilots Fly (Within Reason)

Rules are great—they protect your organization. But the wrong rules may negatively affect your NDI team without protecting anything. One team we know about was working on a cooling technology for ICU patients. The patients and nurses were complaining it caused sores. So the engineering team, having never seen a patient use it and having never used it themselves, decided to get more hands-on.

One of the project leads stripped down to his boxers, lay down, and had the team use the cooling apparatus on him. They learned so much, were proud of it, and presented it to their leadership, saying, "Look, here's what we did, and here's how we know how to improve the product."

Instead of praise, leadership shut them down. "Don't ever do that. We're not accepting the liability of you using it; you're not trained."

Rules are designed to bring subpar people up to an average. But what they often do is take excellent people and drag them down to the average. NDI is about excellence. Any rule that is created to maximize an unhelpful variable (for example, extraneous documentation, irrational governance oversight, draconian liability fears, etc.) should be seriously challenged. Risk and reward are related—if you aggressively squeeze out one, don't be surprised that you've squeezed out the other. So take smart risks. Smart risks have downsides, yes, but they're limited. When a risk with limited downside is paired with a reward of unbounded upside, it is entrepreneurial malpractice not to take it. For risks that could ruin the company, the only rational exposure is no exposure—reward be damned. So next time a risk presents itself, just ask, "Is this a poker hand (at worst, you lose your shirt) or Russian roulette (life is on the line)?" Play poker.

Biding Your Time

Three and a half years before we wrote this book, we started an NDI initiative with a company, and we spent six months identifying new clinical areas of interest for this multibillion-dollar venture with only one product line. They were trying to figure out what other markets and product offerings they could launch, because it's obvious to everyone that a single product company, especially a big one, is risky.

We explained exactly what NDI is, explained the processes, WOMBAT, the piranha method, all that. At the end of Invent, the output blew us away—multiple opportunities emerged that looked even bigger than their current business. Everybody said, "Yes, that's exciting," but the business didn't have the ability to ingest these new ideas and start implementing them. Their core business had too much near-term opportunity to ignore. They were set up as a functional business unit structure in a market they were a long way from fully penetrating. They weren't set up to build anything concurrently. To keep the amazing outputs of NDI alive, their internal team had to get creative.

So we went into hiding for almost a year. First, in the intellectual property department, then slowly expanding to the advanced tech and clinical groups, all the while making steady improvement, putting meat on the bones of what these concepts were, without taking enough of the budget to be noticed. As one of our colleagues, the phenomenally successful medtech innovator Jay Watkins said, "It's not that big companies aren't innovative; it's that the tyranny of the core business keeps them from being innovative." And he's right. In this case, the existing business was growing at a rate of hundreds of millions of dollars a year. Not only was there no urgent reason to deviate from that cash cow, but it was also hilariously illogical to do so.

Despite the risk of being a single-product company, there was simply too much gold right in front of them to look away. That's where the discipline of NDI comes in. Spark, flame, slowly build the fire to a controlled level at which the value becomes self-evident, and then… it's something that would fall above the line.

This may be old hat to you, but in corporate budgeting, there's a concept of things being above the line or below the line. Every year, corporations list all the initiatives, all the things they want to do, and they draw a line. They say that anything below the line, they're not going to fund that year. If it's too big, too costly, too innovative, with long-term payback, it always falls below the line. People's bonuses get paid annually, after all.

Ever hear a question like "Do we even have permission to play in that space?" What a worthless question—who says permission is required? What's implied is that you have to convince that internal stakeholder to grant you permission, and the reality is their opinion means zero. Permission to play is only granted by the market, and external stakeholders in that environment are the ones who articulate what the market's permission to play requires. When you have a solution to the need of the anchor in a way that works for all external stakeholders, you unlock permission to play. Anything else is just a self-imposed constraint out of fear of failure, and fear of failure comes from not having enough proof that you will succeed.

Years with small amounts of funding is the kind of discipline required to get that proof. Rarely is an organization ready to immediately start working on the output of NDI. Transitioning innovative ideas into the intellectual property group is a great way to seek shelter and still build value. Patent life is twenty years, and a project's value and permission to play start to look a lot more impressive when you have ten or more patents on your new innovation. Corporations tie direct value to intellectual property KPIs, and that may just be enough to secure a little more funding for experiments that prove the value of the ideas.

Buy-in for a new idea takes time. The bigger the idea, the more time. The benefit of slowly working away in the background is that other people start to get curious on their own, and that's good for getting total buy-in.

After a couple of years of chipping away, the statue's beauty starts to be easier for others to see. Plus, by that time the company's core ground may start to look a little mined out. When that happens, your yet-to-be-finished masterpiece is ready for prime time, and it has to be above the line.

In the case of this company, they changed their mission statement three years after we started working with them, from managing a particular disease to helping people manage their health. It wasn't just the product line; the whole culture of the company shifted because enough people understood and believed in a new, bigger future. An overnight success . . . three-plus years in the making.

You need to give yourself time to be successful; you need to let the organization—and the people within it—come to their own conclusion. That requires patience—lots of patience—from you. So if you are being held back, plan out where to hide, and we recommend the best place to hide is in a pocket of the organization that is desperate for what you are giving them; intellectual property, advanced technology, or some sort of skunkworks lab for innovation. They typically get half-thought-through ideas thrown over the wall to them and are just told to deal with them. They are used to seeing a lot of half-baked ideas and requests.

So when you show up with a full needs-driven strategy that's not a working product, they're in heaven because creating and protecting the product is their job. And if you prove to them what the value is up front without a fully baked solution, you're not diminishing their value, you're honoring it.

Rewarding Successful Team Members

The unwritten rule in start-ups is that everyone shares in the success through equity. But that's just not reality in some corporations. So unless you want your best NDI people to get poached or become jaded that they built you the next billion-dollar opportunity for a nicely worded performance review, you need to aggressively reward success.

Whatever reward you choose, it has to match the profile of your company and the individuals on the team. If people are only working for you to make money, then cash motivates. If your employees are purpose driven, recognition is more important, similar to promotion, increased responsibility, etc. These things are incredibly motivating but deeply individual.

Our take: give them an opportunity that is highly visible and important in this new multibillion-dollar opportunity they helped create. They might not be the head of it, might not be VP, but they can't go back to being a peon. What kind of message would that send to the next person in line for NDI round two? Going back to the test pilot analogy, the test pilot in the first stealth bomber was chosen to be an astronaut.

Speaking of astronauts, let's talk about those rising stars in your company.

Chapter 9

THE STARS AND STRIPES PARADOX

That's not my job.

The antihero, doing their job

In a start-up—or any small, room-to-grow organization—you're going to have more jobs than you have people for them. You won't be able to afford everything you want to do and you'll have to get very creative. Out of necessity, the people in this group are required to handle several unrelated problems and handle them in a number of different ways. One day you might need someone that can physically repair a piece of machinery, troubleshoot a manufacturing issue, negotiate a contract, followed by rewriting a patent application. When you meet this type of person, you know they are a star.

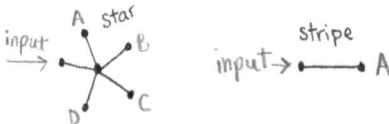

A star is someone who has five or six areas of competency. It's not normal to have that many. Most people discover they are good at one or two things and stick with them. Stars get made because something went *wrong*. They typically have a nontraditional career path, working in construction, then sales, then as a ski instructor, then getting a PhD or MD. (This person knows I'm writing about them.) It doesn't look like it should work, but the skills they accumulate in each domain end up being synergistic in a way that no career counselor would predict and few hiring panels can appreciate. On paper, they look like they come from the Island of Misfit Toys.

Scott Adams, in *How to Fail at Almost Everything and Still Win Big*, would describe people with those interrelated skills as "talent-stacked." In a start-up, you want everyone to be talent-stacked because it's the best way to be nimble while resource-constrained. It's the reason NASA likes astronauts with multiple PhDs because when something in space goes wrong in a new way, you can call for help but it isn't *coming*.

Now, here's what's surprising: these same talent-stacked stars will become *liabilities* as the company matures. If you have a star doing the jobs of four or more people by themselves and then they quit, you're left with an enormous hole to fill in your organization. You could try to fill it with someone who has the same skills as that star. But stars are exceptional rarities and not easy to come by. It's far easier to find two people with three competencies or six people with a single competency. The longer your organization survives, the more often this is going to occur and the most rational choice is to keep transitioning to more traditional talent.

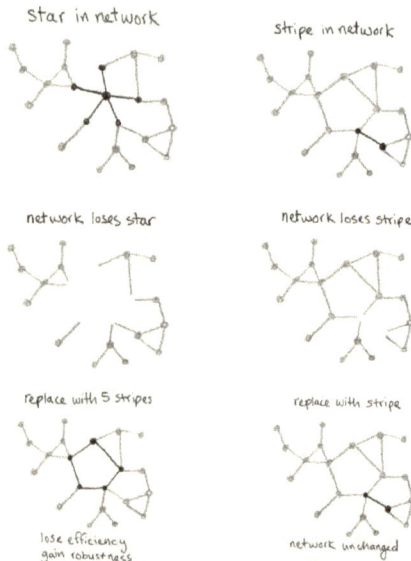

star in network

stripe in network

network loses star

network loses stripe

replace with 5 stripes

replace with stripe

lose efficiency gain robustness

network unchanged

The people with narrower focus that replace the stars are called stripes. They are exceedingly efficient in one or two areas of expertise, consistently handling related tasks efficiently and to a high standard. They are optimized for *execution*, not flexibility.

The process of losing stars and replacing them with stripes, like the Peter principle or Parkinsons' law, is unavoidable without great effort. And unlike those other laws, you probably shouldn't fight it. Losing stars improves the company's safety and efficiency. As the company de-risks its product or service, this is the optimal time to stop exploring and start executing. That stars leave and are replaced with stripes *helps*.

How do you know if your organization is down this path? You'll know you're in a company containing stripes the first time someone responds, "That's not my job." This person is misunderstood as a problem. That's the wrong way to think about it. Stripes are not the problem—they are the highest return on investment for a mature organization. Without the distractions of five or six unrelated tasks, stripes enable companies to scale. When you try to give an unrelated task to a stripe, you are asking them to be worse at their job.

But more is happening than a change in personnel. With a winning product in the market, the march towards executing and optimizing margins does more than swap stars for stripes - it changes the very way that your company works.

Stripes thrive in a rules-based system. As this optimization continues, the company will use rules to ensure that what works keeps working. Taken to its extreme, the company is at risk of codifying all tasks and removing all variance—the same rules that ensure nothing can go terribly wrong also make sure nothing goes surprisingly *right*. This is a true bureaucracy. Without any wiggle room, it becomes very difficult to innovate on product or react to a changing market.

So there is value in remaining flexible, and stripes don't give you that. A stripe's kryptonite is context switching, which innovation demands. Context switching between varied talents is a star's superpower, but it is also what makes them a liability in large organizations. So a *stars and stripes paradox* exists: large organizations have the dollars to invest because they were wildly successful at executing, but continued growth requires innovating in new markets with new products and the right people for that have been steadily selected *against*. That is why start-ups usually outcompete mature organizations when it comes to innovation, because start-ups are where stars have been selected *for*.

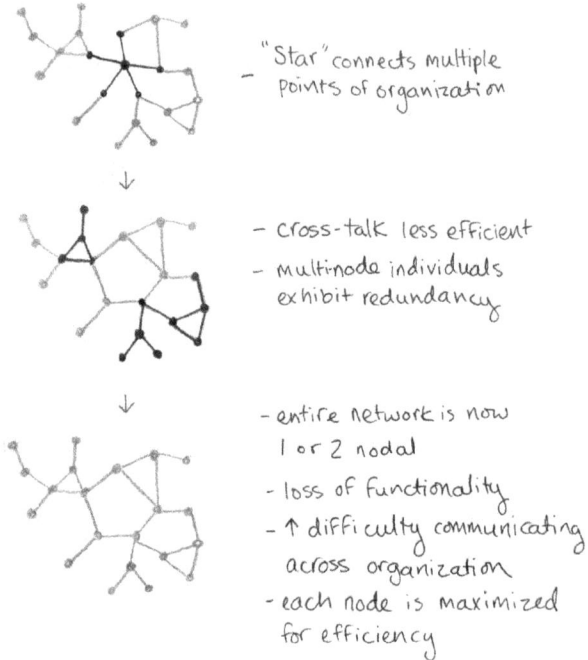

— "Star" connects multiple points of organization

↓

— cross-talk less efficient
— multinode individuals exhibit redundancy

↓

- entire network is now 1 or 2 nodal
- loss of functionality
- ↑ difficulty communicating across organization
- each node is maximized for efficiency

Hiring stars back in is not enough. If your employee, Tim, is talented at electrical and mechanical engineering, a change from one method to the other doesn't bother him. You have flexibility because Tim has flexibility. If Thomas is only skilled in electrical, a change to a mechanical solution means he's fired. Thomas will *resist* this. This is the reality for an organization that tries to innovate with stripes–if you ask rational people to support a change that devalues their abilities, the resistance will be phenomenal and total. Instead, any "innovation" that Thomas suggests will fall neatly into the narrow competency that he already possesses. And any remaining stars will find this environment hostile to *their* competency.

This impulse for stars to leave a bureaucracy is why you'll sometimes see star VPs break a business unit off from the larger corporation, turn it around, and get it reacquired by the parent company. They have to break off because, despite having everything they need to succeed, they're being stopped by internal resistance. Once they remove themselves from the resistance of company culture, the stars can innovate again.

Removal of resistance is key. When Jeff Bezos incubated the Kindle, he did it outside his organization and with an isolated team, protected funding, and separate mission because that kind of innovation could not have happened internally. He had to move outside the stripes with a small team of stars to create that product.

It is important to be intentional. If your goal is innovation then you have to select for that ability, select against resistance, and open up the rules. With some NDI teams, we relocated the team off the main campus for this reason. The members were selected for aptitude, removed from coworkers, and given a high degree of freedom from the existing corporate process. Eventually, things are folded back in and appropriately documented, but the birth is allowed to be messy.

So when you're forming your first or next innovation team, have intention. Be honest about whether you have stripes or stars around. If you try to make a stripe perform as a star, you will be disappointed. If you ask a star to innovate in an environment of stripes, you will be disappointed. It is your responsibility to structure the program for the people you have. Stripes benefit when their roles are clearly defined within an established system. In contrast, stars must be given the freedom to innovate and create as best suits their competencies. If an innovation effort of yours is failing, it is worth taking a close look to see if these issues are at fault.

Chapter 10

NEEDS-DRIVEN INNOVATION, TL;DR EDITION

Tell 'em what you're gonna tell them, then tell them, then tell them what you told them.

—Sadly, the originator of this quote fell into a recursive loop and died

S ome readers of this book will come here first. If that's you, please reconsider. Without proper context, guidance, what-to-do tips, and what-not-to-do warnings, this chapter won't be much help. So turn back to the beginning, then get here when you get here. But if you've read this book sequentially, you are likely ready for a helpful refresher. This is that chapter.

To review, needs-driven innovation contains four unique stages: Inquire, Identify, Invent, and Implement. We'll cover each from a "tl;dr" (too long; didn't read) perspective. Of course, we assume you did read, but the point is made.

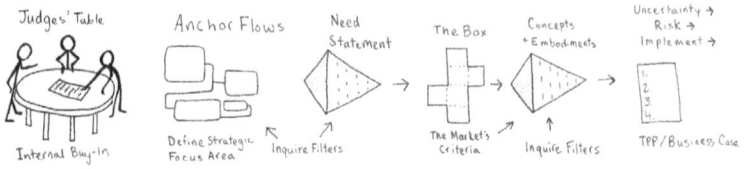

Judges' Table — Internal Buy-In — Anchor Flows — Define Strategic Focus Area — Inquire Filters — Need Statement — The Box — The Market's Criteria — Concepts + Embodiments — Inquire Filters — Uncertainty → Risk → Implement → — TPP / Business Case

Needs-Driven Innovation, Phase I: Inquire

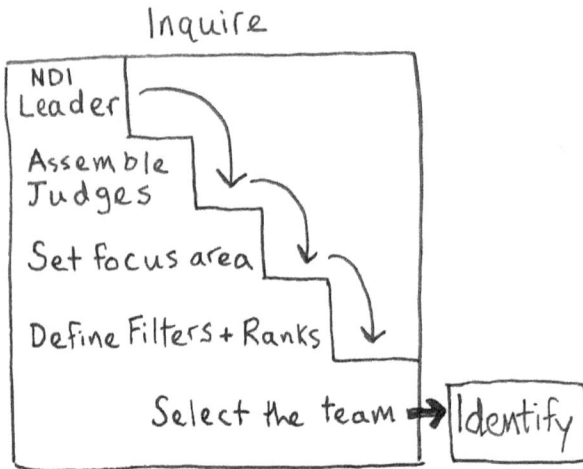

Inquire

NDI Leader
Assemble Judges
Set focus area
Define Filters + Ranks
Select the team → Identify

You are where all this starts—or rather, your belief and desire to change the world. But you can't do it alone. First, you need allies—the most powerful kind—at the top of each function in your organization. These are the judges who rule over the corporate, commercial, and development functions of your business. You must recruit them to support you and then collaborate with them to draw out their filter and rank criteria. These are the criteria on which all NDI projects will be judged as successes or failures.

Once you have secured the criteria and top-down buy-in, it's time to get to work. You'll need a way to observe the anchor stakeholder's need. The anchor is the person or group without which there would be no reason for that industry to exist. Next, you need financial resources, support staff, and an agreed-upon reasonable timeline with little room for contingencies. Last but not least, you need a team of stars—talent-stacked individuals from cross-functional roles who are ready to be your organization's test pilots.

With an area of focus in sight, it's time to let your test pilots fly.

Needs-Driven Innovation, Phase 2: Identify

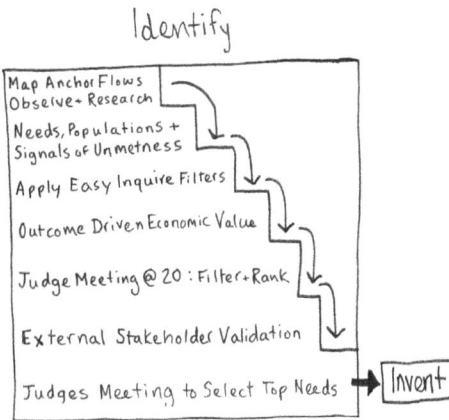

Insights are discovered through direct observation together with deep research into declared and undeclared markets. Zeroing in, you define the external stakeholders: anchor beneficiaries, users, decision-makers, and payers. Observe and research them to accumulate insights into their needs and constraints in different environments. This allows your team to articulate more than a hundred need statements, framed as a way to meet the need for a population. Each need also contains multiple signals of unmetness that will later be qualified into an outcome.

With a hundred-plus need statements in hand, it's time to destroy those not worth your time by applying the filters and ranks you secured from the judges during the Inquire phase. That will take your list down to no more than forty needs that by now have become full need statements with the following structure: "a way to address the need for a homogenous population to reach a valuable outcome."

With a selected outcome and a smaller number of needs to work with, it's time to assign an economic value to each need—a calculation of the financial benefit generated when the need statement is solved. Further prioritization of the highest-value need statements will draw down your list to no more than twenty. The external stakeholders and judges will help you narrow the list further until only a short list of the absolute best need statements remains.

Once you have only a few high-value need statements, it's time to bend metal.

Needs-Driven Innovation, Phase 3: Invent

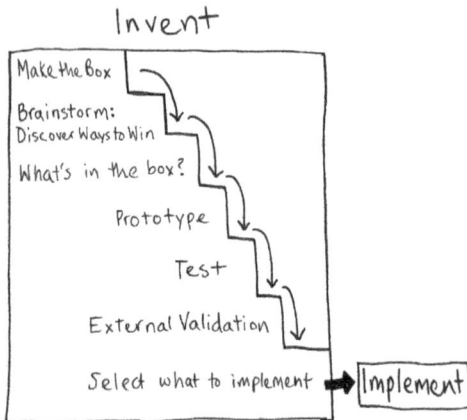

Here, you will think *inside* the box. The box is a set of constraints that any solution must abide by in order to succeed at solving the need statement you so meticulously selected. The walls of the box include the environment where the need will be solved, external stakeholder criteria, competitor benchmarks, financial constraints, execution window, and laws and regulations.

With the box in hand, it's time to discover many ways to win—to create a variety of concepts and then embodiments that will attempt to fit in the box. Only the embodiments that can fit in the box will survive to be filtered and ranked against your other criteria from Inquire. If any embodiments survive, they are viable ideas to solve the need statement.

But you haven't solved anything yet—or even proven that you can. Prototypes must now be built and tested to enable you to validate that you have a winning idea worth implementing.

Needs-Driven Innovation, Phase 4: Implement

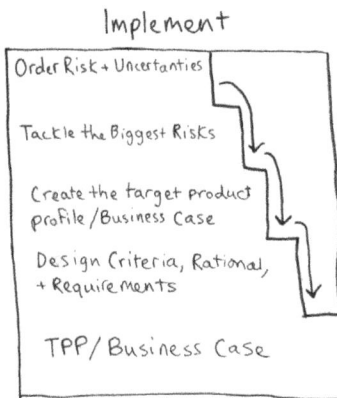

At this point, you have a great unmet need in an unmet market from more than a hundred initial needs. You have validated that it fits the filters and ranks of your judges' criteria as well as the criteria of the external stakeholders. You and the team have designed a box that only excellent ideas fit into. You have prototyped, validated, and tested that you have a winning combination of need statement and embodiment, but you don't yet have a product.

To solve the need, the solution needs to get to the people who need it—the market. The fastest way to get there is to highlight the uncertainty on your journey, understand what risks exist, and then run straight at them. Overcome those hazards or stop. We're not here to WOMBAT.

There will always be people explaining why things cannot be done a certain way. By hook or by crook, get it done. Call in favors, bend leadership, leverage gravitas, or throw money at the obstacles if your process lacks flexibility. Fortune favors the bold. Once the greatest hazards have been minimized, hand it off to the broader organization with their thanks that you've already solved for stakeholder criteria, design requirements, and the needs-driven rationale that justifies them. It will be the easiest—and perhaps most valuable—assignment they've ever seen.

In Summary . . .

Inquire → Identify → Invent → Implement

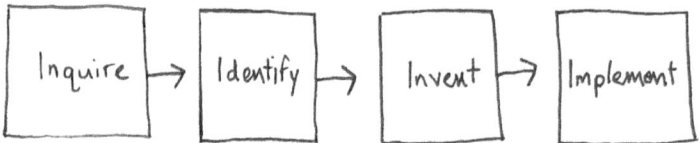

Needs-driven innovation is the method of reverse-engineering to achieve market-product fit. You start with the need and work backward toward the solution. NDI works because it prohibits WOMBAT products that start with an idea and ignore market criteria. Taking this long road of NDI is, in fact, a shortcut that saves both time and money. Otherwise, you'll expend both, only to find that the product built didn't or wouldn't ever satisfy a real need.

The need drives the innovation.

Putting it another way, it's need-solution fit, not product-market fit. And this need is hard won in both its identification and explanation. It is well honed, refined, and researched. This way, your team knows potential market competitors, the criteria they must deliver to those specialized markets, and what corporate parameters their solution must fit to receive maximum stakeholder buy-in.

NDI doesn't create a WOMBAT because it's not a slot machine whose lever you pull, hoping to get lucky by the time your product goes to market. It sounds silly when we put it that way, and yet every non-biodesign/non-NDI-trained team we've encountered follows the gamble-hope-pray-pivot method of innovation.

Needs-driven innovation is tried and true. It just works.

Remember Just Three Things

1. Always start with the need.

Idea generation is fun and exciting. For most people, it's the most enjoyable part of the process. But to lay solid groundwork for needs-driven innovation, the strategy, team-building, market research, and writing of need statements can't be skipped. It's easy to jump ahead and get lost in the idea without setting guardrails to ensure its success. The need must always come first. Even when reversing the process, the magic only happens when you literally reverse your way out of an idea-first dead end. Without a real need, you're just guessing. A real need will push you toward real questions and well-designed constraints that make it impossible to pick anything but a great solution.

2. Just because something works doesn't mean it will *really* work.

Attitudes and priorities matter. The people with the influence to shut down your operation or kill your product before launch may not even know they hold that power. And that is exactly who needs to judge what a workable solution can and cannot look like. They need seats at the table before the plates are even set. Doing this early will prevent monumental disappointment when the great meal of product innovation is brought out, and those with the budget say, "This is not what we ordered!" and it's too late to send it back. This is hard. But it's easier than wasting money, brains, and time on product development that the shot callers in the organization were going to kill anyway.

3. Take your time.

The old saying "A stitch in time saves nine" applies here. We've witnessed innumerable groundbreaking technologies fail at the Implement stage as a result of a poor handoff from prototype to business model execution. It's brutal. Don't do that.

The time taken in each stage—Inquire, Identify, Invent, and Implement—will be time well spent. Even if you feel like you're moving slower than competitors, go ahead and give yourself permission to slow down and be thorough. It's worth it because NDI gives you the ability to see around corners your competitors won't even know exist.

Outro

THE HIDDEN WOMBAT

A serious and good philosophical work could be written consisting entirely of jokes.

—Ludwig Wittgenstein, completely serious

L anguage is a tool for thought and communication. If you don't have a word for something, it's hard to discuss it, think about it, or work on it. In this way, language is not just a tool for your mind to think; it's a tool that expands or shrinks what your mind thinks about.

Sometimes, there is a hole in language and therefore a hole in thought. You notice people stepping in this hole, tripping, and struggling. This book has been aimed at one such hole. We mentioned it earlier in the book, but now we add a finer point.

Look at this figure. On one end, we have things that have zero worth. We have a word for this—worthless. On the other, we have things bursting with worth. We call them worthwhile. What do we call this thing between them?

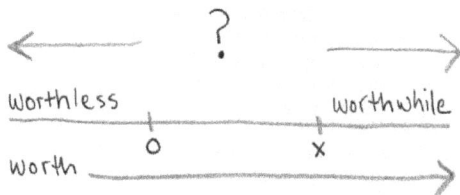

We'll wait.

There is no word for this region of the graph.

The best we could do was *unworthy*, and maybe you're fine with that, but we don't think so. If you're in a conversation with someone about what to do next, what to build, where to spend resources, it causes problems.

Let's say a school has a budget surplus, and they're trying to put the money to good use. The two leading ideas are at a stalemate. "I think we should upgrade all the computers in the school library" versus "I think we should give all the teachers a more competitive salary." Both sides have a dimension they are trying to maximize. Both sides think their approach is worthwhile. Neither side thinks it is unworthy or worthless. What to do?

Anytime you have fewer words than you have things that are different, you're going to get into trouble. Asking *worthless* or *unworthy* to do this job falls short, and it traps the argument—any argument—into one dimension. Without the right word, you cannot focus on the problem. You cannot aim. You are mentally blind.

We offer WOMBAT as the solution to this. WOMBAT is the activity that contains worth but does not meet the necessary threshold for action. WOMBAT is how you lose while you think you're winning. WOMBAT opens a conversation around where and how a threshold (x in the figure) is set. It adds nuance to an area where what we've had up till now has forced black-and-white thinking and silly disagreements.

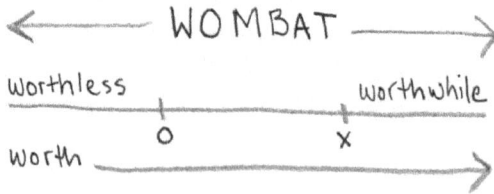

But most importantly, WOMBAT kicks it up a level.

The trigger of money, brains, and time reminds you to consider additional dimensions. Do we have a teacher shortage or trouble with teacher retention? Are the students struggling right now with the computers they have? Are we failing to attract new students to fill each class? Are our students not moving on successfully? The number of dimensions to consider is not infinite, but it is also not one.

This isn't just about business; it's about your life. Where to spend money, brains, and time applies in your family, in your career, in your politics. In each of those arenas, you can feel the difference between productive and contentious conversations. Productivity happens when there is agreement on what the goal is and where the goal is. What exactly are we trying to *do*? Productivity almost never happens when you start with what the solution is. Solution before goal is product before market.

To solve important problems in good faith, you have to discover the dimensions that matter. And with more dimensions, you cannot reconcile them until you have a target that ensures alignment. After all, it's not just "What are we trying to do?" but also "Who are these considerations for?" For us, this is always the anchor stakeholder. Alignment on the anchor and breaking out of single-dimension thinking allow answers to emerge. If you can't agree on the anchor, the effort is adrift.

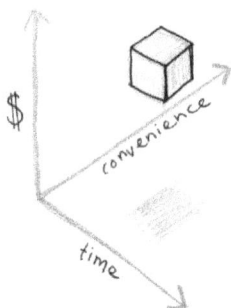

With an anchor set, you can get your bearings. With each dimension, you can start to agree not on an answer, but on a range of acceptable outcomes, starting with a threshold or boundary that must be met. In business, these can be a combination of internal and subjective (Inquire) or external and objective (Invent) thresholds. They define, in this drawing, a literal box. If these three dimensions are all that matter, then anything within this box is a solution, and whatever is outside it, no matter how clever, is WOMBAT. (In practice, there are more than three dimensions, but visually, that's hard to show.)

This is a conversation that you cannot have if a one dimensional figure is your view of the world.

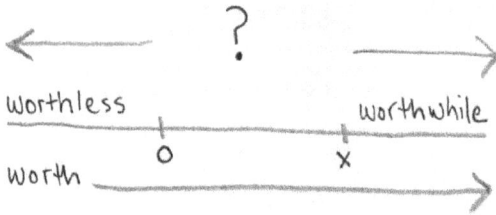

In the same way that full-loop communication is more effortful and more successful than closed loop or open loop, needs-driven innovation is far more effortful and successful than trusting your gut or shooting from the hip.

The reason for needs-driven innovation as a system? Life is short. No matter whether you are working in a big company or founding multiple start-ups, there are only so many shots you have to make an impact in the world. Since it takes five to ten years for a new product to go from a napkin sketch to a mainstream idea, you're lucky to get five chances *in your entire life* to do something that matters.

We want your life's work to be meaningful.

So next time a solution to your problem isn't obviously working, look for the hidden WOMBAT.

We loved writing this book. We hope you loved reading it.

Cheers,

Rush & Topher

ACKNOWLEDGMENTS

From Rush:

To Topher—Thank you—for demanding that we do this and for being an unwavering and open-minded debate partner in search of that perfect prose that has so often eluded me in life. And, to that idiot reviewer on my first research article in graduate school that said "Please have a native English speaker review before resubmission"—check—Thanks Topher.

From Topher:

My thanks to Nicolas Cage, for his thoughtful feedback.

Joint Acknowledgements

First, to acknowledge and thank Joshua Lisec for his patient, thoughtful guidance in the crafting of this book—a true artisan.

Second, to Stanford Byers Center for Biodesign, the entire teaching faculty, our Biodesign Alumni colleagues, and most specifically Paul Yock, Gordon Saul, Lyn Denend, Tom Krummel, and Josh Makower. The most important education we ever received was from you—not just within the Biodesign Fellowship so many years ago but continuing today. The Biodesign Process and your mentorship is the foundation that has enabled us to be successful innovators.

Third, the army of corporate colleagues, collaborators, students, and friends who have been instrumental in guiding how we think about life (and Needs Driven Innovation). This includes all the Biodesign Alumni and thousands more corporate collaborators at large and small companies in the last decade.

Lastly, a special thank you and acknowledgment to these individuals for your time, mentorship, thoughtful comments, or contributing the ideas that became this book: Frank Wang, Saniya Ali, Peter Visconti, Nassir Mokarram, John Paderi, Shaili Sharma, Ladd Suydam, Ashley Jennings, Van Truskett, Kelly Tenbrink, Dimitri Augustin, Ross Venook, John White, Ivan Tzvetanov, Ryan Van Wert, Clay Nolan, Farzad Azimpour, Shriram Raghunathan, Hallie Brinkerhuff, Jannell Ryberg, Travis Ortega, Mitch Muir, Joe Malchar, Marco Mendez, Xavier Salinas, Essence Yung, Matt Johnson, Shirin Tefagh, Ashley Waring, Jonnathan Trexler, Allan Spina, Monica Wylie, Megan Knestrick, Don Mcintosh, Claire Smith, Steve Eichmann, Nick Mourlas, Chuck Scheib, Prasana Malaviya, and the master sherpa who lead us up the Biodesign mountain for the first time—Todd Brinton.

We hope that this book will inspire you to use NDI to make a difference in the lives of others. Thank you all for your support.

ABOUT THE AUTHORS

Rush Bartlett, PhD, MBA

Rush is a five-time startup founder, and corporate executive who has served in CEO, COO, and Chief Product Officer roles at companies ranging from initial founding to more than $150M in revenue. He is also the Associate Director of Corporate Education at Stanford Biodesign and an Executive in Residence at the University of Texas at Austin. He is a prolific inventor with more than one hundred pending and issued patents and was named to Silicon Valley Business Journal's 40 under 40 in 2017. Rush received a BS in Chemical Engineering from the University of Texas, a MBA from Indiana University, and a PhD in Biomedical Engineering from Purdue University. He was a Stanford Biodesign Innovation Fellow in 2012-13. Over the last ten years, he has taught Biodesign to more than 5,000 corporate innovators and has served as an innovation strategy consultant through on-site and remote strategy engagements in North America, Europe, and Asia. His clients have included leading medical technology companies including Abbott, Becton Dickinson, Johnson and Johnson, Edwards Life Sciences, Dexcom, Baxter, Zimmer Biomet, and many more.

Christopher "Topher" Kinsella, MD

Topher is CEO and cofounder of Watershed Therapeutics in addition to a practicing trauma and acute care surgeon. He started his first company, Medalus, during his surgical training at Saint Louis University. He completed the Stanford Biodesign Innovation Fellowship in 2017-18 and adapted the biodesign program for corporate use by standardizing the tools, processes, filters, scoping, and market value analysis. He worked on-site with internal corporate teams, ensuring the adoption of start-up culture and management buy-in for resources. These teams continue to thrive internally without the need for external support. Topher joined Life Science Angels to support due diligence and screening for start-ups. He is now taking what he learned from the clinic, the deal room, and the classroom into his own start-up from napkin to first in human.

www.ingramcontent.com/pod-product-compliance
Lightning Source LLC
Chambersburg PA
CBHW021459180326
41458CB00051B/6879/J